Côte d'Azur

GW00578308

Daniel Anker

Côte d'Azur

Translated by Gill Round

44 selected valley and mountain walks and a longdistance path
in the Maritime Alps, the Haut Pays Grassois, the Estérel,
the Massif des Maures, on the Côtes varoise,
between Toulon and Marseille and in the Calanques

With 79 colour photographs, 44 walking maps
to a scale of 1: 50 000, 1: 75 000 and 1: 100 000
as well as an overview map to a scale of 1: 1 000 000

ROTHER · MUNICH

Front cover:
Blue, white, red – and green: the GR des Balcons de la Côte d'Azur in the Calanques (Walk 42).

Frontispiece (photo on page 2):
You can't get any further: with the Rocher de St-Baume the Alps drop away into the sea (Walk 21).

All photographs by the author except for pages 49 and 79 (Eva Feller).

Cartographie:
Walking maps to a scale of 1: 50 000 / 1: 75 000 / 1: 100 000
and overview maps to a scale of 1: 1 000 000 / 1: 2 000 000
© Bergverlag Rother Munich
(drawn by cartographer Christian Rolle, Holzkirchen)

Translation: Gill Round

1st edition 2001
© Bergverlag Rother GmbH, Munich

ISBN 3-7633-4817-4

Distributed in Great Britain by Cordee, 3a De Montfort Street, Leicester
Great Britain LE1 7HD, www.cordee.co.uk
in USA by AlpenBooks, 3616 South Road, C-1, Mukilteo, WA 98275
USA, www.alpenbooks.com

ROTHER WALKING GUIDES

Azores · Côte d'Azur · Crete West · Cyprus · Gran Canaria · Iceland · La Palma · Madeira · Mallorca · Mont Blanc · Norway South · Provence · Sardinia · Sicily · High Tatra · Tenerife · Tuscany North · Valais East · Around the Zugspitze

Dear mountain lovers! We would be happy to hear your opinion and suggestions for amendment to this Rother Walking guide.

BERGVERLAG ROTHER · Munich
D-85521 Ottobrunn · Haidgraben 3 · Tel. 0049/89/608669-0 · Fax -69
Internet http://www.rother.de · **E-mail** bergverlag@rother.de

Preface

The walks in this guide are on the most famous coastline in Europe, perhaps even of the world. Every bay and every grove, every village and every slope seems to show clear signs of mass tourism and in July and August people swarm together like insects on the French Riviera – the playground of the rich, the beautiful (or those who would like to be) and the extreme right National Front.

On eight separate journeys we discovered a different Côte d'Azur where it still remains true to its name, the 'azure-blue coast'. In autumn, for example, we were on Cap Camarat near the famous beaches of St. Tropez when the trendy restaurants had long pulled down their shutters. Twice we were away for the whole of June and discovered the barren highlands of Grasse, dominated by Montagne du Cheiron (1778) with its 1000m high south flank where mountain farmers had formerly built their high terraces. Once in February we were at the coast as snow storms swept across the rest of the Alps. Blossoming mimosa lined our path as we walked, in shorts, along a pilgrims' trail towards a chapel dating from the 12th century. Two days later we made our way across icy paths onto the St. Baume mountain range from where we looked down over Provence. Another time in April we left Toulon by bus in dull, drizzly weather and a flourishing world of aromas, colours and sea awaited us at Cap Sicié. And then there's Porquerolles, that island in front of Hyères where you can swim, walk and go cycling. The first time we went to the largest of the Îles d'Or we only stayed for a day. On our next visit we treated ourselves to a room in the 'Auberge les Glycines' and when we returned, we rented an apartment right by the harbour. If ever we take the boat again to Porquerolles we will just buy a one way ticket.

Then we did the whole coast again at break neck speed. We took the night train from Geneva to Nice, walked from Menton via St. Agnès, the highest coastal village in France, to La Turbie, and went down to Monaco by taxi in the pouring rain. And after that we did la traversée des Calanques from Cassis to Marseille. Once in Callelongue after a 10 hour hike, we could have taken the bus, but we continued with our rucksacks and left harbours, cars, houses and fortresses behind. We took a marked path through the stony green countryside and breathed in the smell of pine trees and thyme, and with views of the Mediterranean, all the way. It's the most western path of the Calanques, the last section of the *GR of the Balcons de la Côte d'Azur*, and it's called the *Sentier du Président.*

Bern, winter 2000/2001   Daniel Anker

Contents

Tourist tips from azure blue sea to zigzag paths

Grade: beach walks to summit walks

Most of the walks introduced here on the Côte d'Azur are on marked paths, either red and white for the *sentier de Grande Randonnée (GR)*, or yellow for the *petit sentier* (small path). The coastal path, the *sentier littoral*, is usually marked yellow as well. Sure-footedness and a head for heights are just as important inland as on the coast. The walks are given different colours in order to be able to identify the grade at a glance. They are as follows:

BLUE

These paths are well marked, usually comfortably broad, hardly exposed and only moderately steep. They do not require previous mountain experience and can usually be undertaken with relatively little danger in bad weather. These walks rarely take longer than 4 hours.

RED

These paths are adequately marked, but sometimes narrow and exposed. There are certain sections which have been protected. Some sure-footedness and fitness is required and a head for heights, and suitable equipment including good footwear is always essential. The walking time can be as much as 8 hours.

BLACK

These trails and mountain paths – sometimes marked (perhaps even as official paths), but sometimes not – are really only suitable for sure-footed, fit and experienced mountain walkers with a head for heights. You might even have to use your hands in certain steep and rocky areas. This applies also to the red-marked paths in the Calanques, where even the normal paths are a half to a full grade more difficult than is usual between Menton and Marseille.

Public transport: train, bus, boat

All locations, starting points and destinations of the 44 day walks described in this guide as well as the long distance path of *'the blue horizon'* from Menton to Marseille are accessible by public transport. The network of trains, busses and boats is not as densely developed as, for example, in Switzerland. Unfortunately there is no complete timetable of all the possible routes, and so the use of public transport tends to be rather difficult for anyone unfamiliar with the area and with little knowledge of French.

Here are a few tips:

■ At larger train stations there are free individual timetables, for example, those of the Transports Alpes-Maritimes [TAM] in the Département of the same name. The 'Guide régional des transports' has proved to be very useful, as well as the small timetables, eg. for the Vintimille – St. Raphaël line (with all regional trains). Sometimes you have to copy down the local timetables at each stop. Gare SNCF de Nice, tel: 04 36 35 35 35 or 04 93 87 50 50. Gare SNCF de Toulon, tel: 04 94 91 50 50. Gare SNCF St.Charles de Marseille, tel: 04 91 08 50 50.

■ You can obtain timetables for buses in the bus station (Gare Routière) in larger towns. Gare Routière de Menton, tel: 04 93 35 73 91. Gare Routière de Nice, Promenade du Paillon (20 minutes from the train station along Av. Jean Médecin and Av. Félix Faure), tel: 04 93 85 61 81. Gare Routière de Grasse, tel: 04 93 36 49 61 or 04 93 36 37 37. Gare Routière de Marseille, Place Victor Hugo (near to the train station), tel: 04 91 08 16 40.

■ Timetables are often obtainable from the Office du Tourisme or Syndicat d'Initiative (both mean tourist office).

■ On Sundays and Bank Holidays the bus services are rather thin, if they run at all.

■ As a rule each walk gives details of where you can get information.

Chemin de fer: with the 'TGV Méditerranée' within 3 hours from Paris to Marseille
Four railway lines, two big and two small, go down to the southeast coast of France: 1. from Germany/Switzerland via Milano, Genova and Ventimiglia to Nice (eg. direct connections from Basel to Nice), 2. from Switzerland via Torino, Cuneo, the Tenda pass and Sospel to Nice, 3. from France/Switzerland via Grenoble and the Col de la Croix Haute to Digne and then on the Train des Pignes ('fir cone train') of the Chemin de Fer de Provence to Nice, 4. from France/Switzerland (Paris/Geneva) via Lyon and Avignon through the Rhône valley down to Marseille and Nice. From June 2001 the high speed train 'TGV Méditerranée' will take only 3 hours from Paris to Marseille, and 6½ hours from Geneva to Nice – it's almost as fast as going by plane and certainly quicker than by car. There are numerous trains between Ventimiglia and Marseille, one of the most beautiful train journeys in the world: TGV, express and stopping trains. Train enthusiasts can travel to Sospel on the Tenda train and return on the Train des Pignes.

Length of time: up to the nearest ¼ of an hour
The times are based on a walking speed of about 4km on hour over level ground or up to about 300m ascent under normal conditions. They do not include stops for swimming and eating etc.

Food and drink: baguette and Bandol
There are plenty of opportunities for buying food in most villages (except perhaps in the middle of the off-peak season), on Sundays too in the larger places. The boulangerie is usually open and you can buy a croissant or a

pain au chocolat here. It's best to take some food with you on the walks unless the path goes past a beach café. You should also take enough fluids and you can refill your drinks bottles at the village spring. A good accompaniment to a picnic of local delicacies (pâté, cheese, dried tomatoes) is of course a bottle of Côtes de Provence, Bandol, Cassis or Bellet (the wine of Nice). Bon appétit et à votre santé!

Guides (in French): available from kiosques and Maisons de la Presse

- Detailed guides (with good map sketches) written by Alexis Lucchesi from the publishers Edisund (Aix-en-Provence) are very useful and cover the following areas: Estérel, Maures, Côte Varoise et les Îles d'Or, Sainte-Baume, Calanques.

Refreshing all the senses: picnic spot in the Calanque d'En Vau. Please take empty bottles away with you.

- Interesting books describing shorter walks from the series 'petites traces vertes' of the Editions Didier Richard (Grenoble). Each of the 52 family walks go into the Pays Niçois, into the surrounding area of Cannes and Grasse, Toulon and Hyère as well as round Marseille.

- Official topo guides of the Fédération française de la randonnée (Paris), which cover every GR, often cover the petites randonnées too. Recommended guides are the *Balcons de la Méditerranée* (GR 51 from Menton to Marseille, out of print), Massifs Provençaux (GR 9, 98 and 90 with Sainte-Victoire, Sainte-Baume, Maures, Calanques), La Côte Varoise et les Îles.

- *Circuits pédestres du guide franck* (Annecy) with individual removable sheets (walk description and map) for the Pays Varois, Alpes Maritime.

- Picture guides of the collection '*Montagne-Randonnée*' of the Edition Glénat (Grenoble): *Les Balcons de la Côte d'Azur* (Maritime Alps as far as Estérel) by Michel Bricola and *Les Sentiers des Calanques* by Jean-François Devaud.

- Other recommendations are both the volumes of Jean Bérenguier on the Estérel and the Golfe de St. Tropez (*Promenez-vous à pied...* series), the leaflets on the walking opportunities in Coaraze and suggestions for walks in the glossy pages of Pays de Provence – Côte d'Azur and the Alpes magazine.

Use of the guide: an almost continuous network of day walks
The walks have been chosen so that the destination of one walk is the same as the start of the following one. In this way there has evolved a loose-knit network of paths on the Côte d'Azur and in its hinterland, combining all the necessary tourist information.

Ascent: and remember that the descent is also important
Ascents and descents are given where they are different. Not only uphill climbing is demanding of strength and stamina, but so are steep descents – and sometimes long stretches over level sand. The height details come mainly from the IGN map 1: 25 000.

Information: addresses of tourist offices

General
www.franceguide.com (main website with links to regional internet pages)
Comité Régional du tourisme Provence-Alpes – Côte d'Azur, Les Docks, 10 place de la Joliette, F-13567 Marseille Cedex 02, tel: 04 91 56 47 00, fax: 04 9 156 47 01, e-mail: crtprov@wanadoo.fr
Comité Régional du Tourisme Riviera Côte d'Azur, 55 promenade des Anglais, BP 602, 06011 Nice Cedex 1, tel: 04 93 37 78 78, fax: 04 93 86 001 06, e-mail: crt06@crt-riviera.fr, internet: www.crt-riviera.fr
Comité Départementale du Tourisme du Var, B.P.99, 83303 Draguignan, tel: 04 94 50 55 50, fax: 04 94 50 55 51, service documentation tel: 04 94 50 55 65
Comité Départementale du Tourisme des Bouches-du-Rhône, 13 rue Roux de Brignoles, 13006 Marseille, tel: 04 91 13 84 13, fax: 04 91 33 01 82, internet: www.visitprovence.com

Offices de tourisme according to regions
Nice: 06500 Menton, tel: 04 92 41 76 76, fax: 04 92 41 76 78
06000 Nice, tel: 04 93 92 82 82, fax: 04 93 92 82 98
06380 Sospel, tel: 04 93 04 15 80, fax: 04 93 04 19 36
Grasse: 06130 Grasse, tel: 04 93 36 66 66, fax: 04 93 36 86 36
06400 Cannes. tel: 04 93 39 24 53, in the station tel: 04 93 99 19 77
06140 Tourrettes-sur-Loup, tel: 04 93 24 18 93, fax: 04 93 59 24 40
Estérel: 83702 Saint-Raphaël cedex, tel: 04 94 19 52 52, fax: 04 94 83 85 40
Maures:
83230 Bormes-les-Mimosas, tel: 04 94 71 15 17, fax: 04 94 64 79 57
83680 La Garde-Freinet, tel: 04 94 43 67 41, fax: 04 94 43 08 69

83610 Collobrières, tel: 04 94 48 08 00, fax: 04 94 48 05 62.
Côte varoise:
    83240 Cavalaire-sur-Mer, tel: 04 94 01 92 20, fax: 04 94 05 49 89
    83420 La Croix-Valmer, tel: 04 94 55 12 12, fax: 04 94 55 12 10
    83400 Hyères, tel: 04 94 01 84 50, fax: 04 94 01 84 51
    83400 Porquerolles, tel: 04 94 58 33 76, fax: 04 58 36 39
    83400 Port-Cros, Centre d'Information du Parc National,
    tel: 04 94 05 90 17
    83990 St-Tropez, tel: 04 94 97 45 21, fax: 04 94 97 82 66
Between Toulon and Marseille:
    83000 Toulon, tel: 04 94 18 53 00, fax: 04 94 18 53 09
    83150 Bandol, tel: 04 94 29 41 35, fax: 04 94 32 50 39
    13260 Cassis, tel: 04 42 01 71 17, fax: 04 42 01 28 31
    13000 Marseille, tel: 04 91 13 89 00, fax: 04 91 13 89 20

Great Britain:
French Government Tourist Office, 178, Piccadilly, W1J9AL London, tel:
09068 244 123, fax: 207 493 65 94, e-mail: info@mdlf.co.uk

Season: avoid high summer
There are only two months to avoid the Côte d'Azur – July and August –
when it's too full, too hot, too dry and too loud!

■ **Best walking season:** April to June when all the flowers are out, the
hotels and museums are open and everything is possible except perhaps
swimming in the sea which can be a bit chilly. But in April and May the
weather is not as consistent and you can expect rain showers. In June the
sky is normally blue, the gorse is flowering and sometimes it is beautifully
warm on the mountains by the coast. And then there's spring when the
mimosa trees are full of yellow blossom and the skies are blue. Nothing
but occasional gray clouds! And in October and November when lots of
hotels, restaurants and shops are closed, the autumn leaves are still on
the trees and the last flowers are still blossoming. Even this season has its
own special attraction. Only swimmers are bothered if the Mistral is blowing, not the randonneurs.

■ **Festivals:** in the second half of February there's a carnival in Nice and the
lemon festival in Menton.

■ **Hunting season:** it is recommended that you wear colourful clothes in
September.

■ **Danger of forest fires:** another reason why walking should be avoided in
high summer: when there's a danger of forest fires certain paths might be
blocked off (for example, in the Massif des Maures). It's forbidden to walk
through the forests and undergrowth in the Département Bouches-du-
Rhône from the 1st of July to the second Saturday in September, except

Tranquillity before the height of the tourist season: a rest on the summit of Port Cros (Walk 20).

the paths on the coast, eg. a few in the Calanques like the *Sentier de la Douane* and the path from Cassis to En Vau. The fire-protected roads are not walking paths, nor is it pleasant to walk along these firebreaks although this is your only option sometimes. Because of the risk of fires it is important to remember that it is forbidden to light a fire along these paths and smoking is often prohibited too.

■ **Météo:** weather forecasts are in accordance with each département, tel: 08 36 68 02 plus both numbers of the Département: 06 for the Alpes Maritimes, 13 for Bouches-du-Rhône, 83 for Var. The weather forecast can be found in the *Nice Matin* and *Var matin* newspapers.

Maps: TOP 25 is really first class

The three Didier Richard maps, scale 1: 50 000, with marked walks (randonnées pédestres) are sufficient to start with: sheets 24 (Collines provençales), 25 (Les Maures et le Haut Pays Varois), 26 (Au pays d'Azur).

If you want maps for hiking then look out for the blue IGN maps in the TOP 25 series (scale 1: 25 000). Not only are the paths marked in red but also various other tourist information. The maps can normally be bought on the way in the Maisons de Presse, or sometimes in good bars.

Literature: *Afloat* is a must

- Guy de Maupassant, *Sur l'Eau*, the classic of 1988 which was published in a wonderful edition in 1995 under the title *Afloat*.
- Mary Blume, *Côte d'Azur. Inventing the Rivièra*, 1992. A bit heavy for the rucksack but a must for reading on the beach with its entertaining account of why men and women lie by the azure-blue sea.
- Nicole Williams: *Provence & the Côte d'Azur*, Lonely Planets Publications. A must for the rucksack.
- Katherine Mansfield: *The Journal 1904-1922*. The author lived and worked in the Hotel Beau Rivage in Bandol in 1915 and 1918.
- Patrick Robinson: *Masquerade in Port-Cros*. A Romance of the Côte d'Azur. O là là.

Equipment: sandals and walking poles

For the coastal path around Cap Ferrat, the stroll to Porquerolles beaches or the walk over the Croisette in Cannes, sandals are perfectly adequate. Otherwise sturdy walking shoes are recommended and ready worn swim-wear (you don't even need this on the Plage de Pampelonne). Sun protection, rainwear and mini-bank card are equally essential, as well as enough fluids. Long trousers and walking poles are an advantage when going through bushes on more difficult walks.

Protection of nature and the environment: look after the alpine coast

1. Don't leave any pollution behind, exhaust fumes or litter.
2. Protect animals and plants.
3. Show respect for local inhabitants and their property.
4. Stay on marked paths.
5. Don't smoke or light fires along the paths.
6. Camping is not permitted other than in designated areas.

Route finding: left is not always immediately left

The direction details left and right are used for the direction in which you are walking. However the expressions on the right hand side of the valley and on the right hand bank are looking down stream. The names are given in accordance with the IGN maps 1: 25 000 or the guides.

Private property: no entry

Propriété privée is wide-spread on the Côte d'Azur. What looks like a track, path or little road on the map and should be accessible, is in fact not: either it is private, fenced off or signed no thoroughfare. Signs and similar markings often indicate clearly that entry is forbidden. If you keep to the official paths (*GR*, *sentier littoral* etc.) you will not be surprised by fierce dogs, although you can use more paths than those indicated on the tourist walking maps.

Rescue: au secours!

Police, tel: 17

Fire brigade, tel: 18

There is a police station in almost every village. Mountain rescue is called in French: secours en montagne.

Sport: only swimming is nicer

■ **Canyoning:** next to the Pyrenees, the hinterland of the Côte d'Azur is the finest area in Europe. In the Alpes Maritimes there are numerous wild gorges. More information can be obtained from: Loc-Aventure, 13 rue Fontaine de la Ville, 06300 Nice, tel: 04 93 56 14 67 and *L'Aventure Verticale dans les Alpes d'Azur*, by C. and J.P.Sounier, Edisud 1992.

Walkers allowed: a generous sign in the hinterland (Walk 14).

■ **Climbing:** the IGN map 909 *France. Sîtes naturels d'escalade* provides a good overview. And with the following guides you could be occupied for more than a few weeks: Jean-Claude Raibaud: *L'escalade dans les Alpes-Maritimes*; Christian Rive: *Escalade dans les Maures et l'Estérel*; Denis Garnier: *Escalades autour de Toulon*; Bignon/Fenouil/Frisque/Lucchesi: *Sélection d'Escalades dans les Calanques*. Information: Bureau des guides de la Côte d'Azur, tel: 04 93 39 64 77, fax: 04 93 68 22 88. Another place to go is Marie Cord' in St-Jeannet (Walk 11).

■ **Cycling:** one example: the Estérel massif and coast are excellent for cycling (a mountain bike would be on advantage). The highest summit of the Estérel is just as manageable as some of the deep gorges. During the day the coast road is quite busy, but the rest of the roads and paths offer pure delight on two wheels.

Trekking: paths of the Grande Randonnée (GR)

GR 51 Sentier de Grande Randonnée 'les Balcons de la Côte d'Azur', part of the European long distance path E7 from Zagreb to Lissabon. At the start it follows the *'Alta Via dei Monti Liguri'* (Walk 45).

GR52 and *5* from Valdeblore through the Mercantour National Park to Sospel and on to Menton. It is the alpine alternative to the *GR 5* (which is also the long distance path from Amsterdam to Nice) as well as the continuation of the Italian GTA (which comes from Monte Rosa) to the Mediterranean (Walks 1,10, 45).

The *GR 510 Le Sentier des Huit Vallées* crosses the eight valleys of Beil-sur-Roya in the Nice hinterland to St-Cézaire-sur-Siagne (Walks 17,18).

GR 4 and *49*: both the GRs run from Provence to Grasse (Walk 16) and St.Raphaël respectively. There's more on this in the topo guide of the FFRP *De la Méditerranée aux gorges du Verdon*.

GR 9, 98 and *90*: the *GR 9* comes from the north down to the Méditerranée and goes across the Massif de Sainte-Baume and the Massif des Maures to St-Pons-les-Mûres west of St. Tropez (Walks 24, 37). Two paths branch off from this and are highly recommended: the *GR 98*, which descends from Saint-Baume to Cassis and then goes through the Calanques to Marseille (Walks 38, 42), as well as the *GR 90* which reaches Le Lavandou from Notre-Dames des Anges (Walk 45, alternative).

Accommodation: hotels, gîtes d'étapes and campsites

Details of accommodation have been given, wherever possible with telephone numbers and other important information. Most accommodation offers meals as well. The list of hotels for the Provence-Alpes – Côte d'Azur region is very useful as well as the 'Hôtels de tourisme' (available from the Comités Régionaux de Tourisme amongst other places). The Département Alpes Maritimes, Var and Bouches-du-Rhône distribute their own hotel lists. As a rule you cannot go wrong with the hotels which belong to the Logis de France, centre for reservations tel: 04 93 80 80 40. The logis of Provence-Alpes – Côte d'Azur are accessible on the internet: http//www.logis-de-france.com. For overnight accommodation, youth hostels and huts it's best to get a copy of the *Gîtes d'étapes et Refuges* by Annick and Serge Mouraret, which covers the whole of France and neighbouring countries (Editions La Cadole, F-78140 Vélizy, ISBN 2-908567-06-7), www.gites-refuges.com.

For camping the camping guide for the region Provence-Alpes – Côte d'Azur has proved to be very helpful as well as the Michelin *Camping Caravaning France*. You can take campers and caravans onto most campsites. If you are looking for something more modest choose Camping à la ferme (farm campsites).

Organisations and clubs: excursions on foot

Guided walks on the Côte d'Azur are (still) quite rare. Apparently tourists prefer to swim rather than walk.

You can write to the following French walking organisations:

Fédération française de randonnée pédestre FFRP, 14, rue Riquet, 75019 Paris, tel: 01 44 89 93 93, fax: 01 40 35 85 67, www.ffrp.asso.fr.

Comité Départemental de la Randonnée Pédestre, 2 rue Gustave Deloye, 06000 Nice, tel: 04 93 09 91 27.

Société des excursionnistes marseilles, 16 rue Rotonde, 13001 Marseille, tel: 04 91 84 75 52.

Paths: red and white, yellow and multi-coloured
In the Département of Alpes-Maritime the marked paths usually have numbered signs. The numbers are also on the IGN series Top 25 so that you always know where you are. In both the other Départements there are – with the exception of the yellow-marked *sentier littoral* – few signs. If there are no markings present or if they are so colourful that they are of no help, you should read the map. Difficulties arise because of private property.

The *GRs* are good, but they are not always clearly marked red and white. If the paint marks intersect you are not on the *GR* any more. The *petits sentiers* have broad yellow paint marks.

Tip: narrow green paint marks on a white background indicate the boundary of a national forest (forêt dominiale)

Zigzaguer: do you speak French?
I do not wish the users of this guide any confusion either on the coastal path round Cap St. Tropez nor in the narrow streets of the old town of St.Tropez itself. If you are able to understand more than 'bonjour' and 'au revoir' it would be a great help to you between Marseille and Menton. Anyway, whether you do or not – une belle balade!

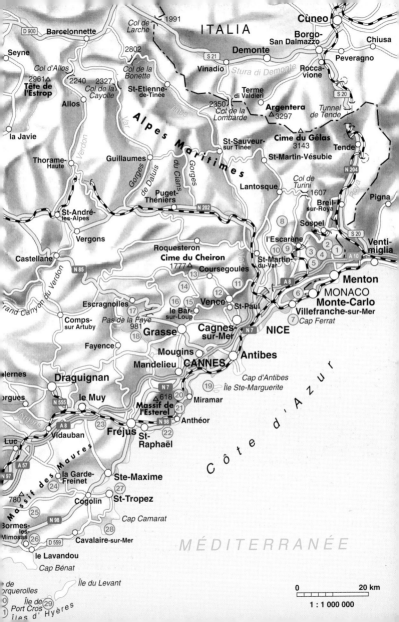

Between Menton and Nice: the Maritime Alps

'The wall of the Alps rises up here out of the blue waves of the sea as bright as the goddess Aphrodite to defend central Europe from sea-borne attacks'. This is how Ludwig Purtscheller, one of the German speaking discoverers of the Alpes Maritimes, evoked the distinctiveness of the Alpes Maritimes in his posthumously published work *Über Fels and Firn* in 1901. Here is the section of the alpine arc that is finally washed ashore 'by the blue waves of the Ligurian Sea'. Although the waves are not often to be seen. 40 kilometres behind the Côte d'Azur there's nothing to remind one of the mild Mediterranean landscape. Here are the same barren primary rocks as to be found in the Gotthard mountains, the heart of the Alps, granite slabs and scree, sharply serrated ridges and sparse vegetation. Mont Clapier (3045m), the southern-most 3000er of the Alps, towers over the border between France and Italy. Somewhat further behind the Cime du Gélas from whose north flank a Mediterranean glacier emerges in its last death throes.

The landscape on the alpine shore is quite different and doesn't want to comply with our picture of the Alps. The idyllic wilderness behind Monte Carlo is arid ground, thorny plants, blossoming lemon and olive trees on terraced slopes. A walk on the seaward side of the Maritime Alps can certainly become a roulette of tarmac roads, clusters of villas and remains of mule tracks, accompanied by the barking of dogs and fig trees from which to pinch some fruit. But if you keep to the accurately marked *long distance path no. 51* 'Les Balcons de la Côte d'Azur' (Walks 4, 5, 9 and 10) you will not lose your way between Menton and Nice, the eastern part of the azure-blue coast. The first belvedere is Plan de Leuze, rising 700m vertically above the yacht harbour of Menton. Here, ruins of farmhouses, fields separated by dry stone walls and full of gorse and red flowers, sit above the sea. In the distance you can see the sea of houses in Monte Carlo and above the Roc d'Orméa, the first (or last) summit of the Alps. It's a beautiful place, just like Sainte-Agnès, where you look down over the start of the Côte d'Azur from the terrace of the restaurant 'Le Righi'.

In La Turbie stands the immense Trophée des Alpes, in memory of the conquest of the alpine people, erected at the 503rd milestone on the later Via Aurelia from Rome to Nîmes and Narbonne. At this historical point the imperial road crosses the last, 'azure' section of the transALPedes. This was an ecological march which went from Vienna to Nice in the summer of 1992 in 122 days, to draw attention to the destruction of the Alps and its people, and to fight against it.

That the summit above La Turbie is called Mont de la Bataille is no coincidence. It is not the only 'battle mountain' between Menton and Nice. You can often find military evidence right up to the summit, as for example on Mont Razet (Walk 2) and Mont Chauve d'Aspremont, the local mountain of Nice

Coup de foudre: the climb from Menton to the first belvedere on the azureblue coast makes your heart beat faster. And how!

(Walk 10). The southern part of the Alpes Maritimes was strongly contested in the 2nd World War. The Authion ridge was the last part of France to be liberated from the German occupying forces (on the 25th April 1945).

No (war time or agricultural) ruins, almost no ugly (tourist) buildings accompany the walk round the peninsular of Cap Ferrat, only delightful villas in prime positions. You can admire them from outside – and inside (Walk 7). Both the other coastal walks in this area of the Côte d'Azur, Cap Martin and Cap d'Ali, are less worthwhile – not least because there aren't so many idyllic places. And what would coastal walks be like if there were no opportunities for swimming?

To walk along the coast involves not only horizontal but uphill travel and the walker is constantly moving from one to the other. You look down onto the sea of houses in Monaco and Nice and then behind them, to the other sea. This is the Caribbean of the turn of the century, where the wealthy tourists wintered in the Côte d'Azur sun like the philosopher Nietzsche who spent five winters in Nice between 1883 and 1888. The cleverly built path from Èze-Bord-de-Mer through the steep rocks up to the village of Èze is dedicated to him. You walk twice along the *Sentier Frédéric Nietzsche* on the descent (Walks 5 and 6). And then you can bathe your feet in the Mediterranean.

1   Roc d'Orméa, 1132m

The first (or last) summit of the alpine arc

Sospel – Col du Razet – Colla Bassa – Baisse de Fayche Fonda – Col de Berceau – Roc d'Orméa – Plan de Lion – Menton-Garavan

Starting point: Sospel (348m) on the train line Cuneo – Tende – Breil-sur-Roya – Nice. Sospel train station, tel: 04 93 04 00 17; buses from Nice and Menton; Transports Rey, tel: 04 93 04 01 24.
Destination: Menton-Garavan (0m). Compare Walk 4.
Walking times: Sospel – Col du Razet 2½ hours, Col du Razet – Roc d'Orma 2 hours, summit – sea 1 ½ hours. Total time 6 hours.
Ascent: 1080m, descent 1440m.
Distance: 15km.
Grade: All the way on the white and red marked *GR 52* up to the summit climb where you need to use your hands.
Best time of year: All year round.
Refreshments and accommodation: In Sospel: Auberge du Pont Vieux, tel: 04 93 04 00 73; Gîte d'étape Le Mercantour and Hôtel des Etrangers, tel: 04 93 04 00 09; Camping

Mas Fleury, tel: 04 93 04 03 48. In Menton: compare Walk 4.
Alternative: From the Colla Bassa you can climb straight up the yellow marked path across the eastern flank to the stony summit memorial of the Grand Mont (1379m), which is on the border. In Italy this summit between Sospel and Menton is called Monte Grammondo. The descent either goes back to the Colla Bassa or along the mule track on the Italian side below the border ridge as far as the Pas de la Come, over which you return to France. About 1 hour longer.
Places of Interest: La mer d'azur.
Map: TOP 25: Vallée de la Bévéra (3741 ET), Nice – Menton (3742 OT).
Tip: Jardin des Colombières in Menton-Garavan: open daily except Sunday 10-12.00, 15-17.00, tel: 04 93 35 71 90.
Adjoining walks: 2, 4, 45.

Where does the alpine arc rise up out of the Mediterranean? Is it at the Trophée des Alpes above Monaco, the Roman memorial which was erected in 6 BC in memory of the resistance of the alpine people? Hardly, nor is it at Mont Agel (1448) which lies nearby, the highest mountain directly above the Côte d'Azur, but unfortunately inaccessible since the extensive summit plateau is covered with mysterious constructions. The remaining contender is the long ridge between France and Italy which drops down from the Gros Mont uninterrupted into the azure-blue sea. The southern-most rise on this ridge which can be described as a summit is the Cime de Restaud. Separated from it by the Col du Berceau (the col of the cradle) is the towering Roc d'Orméa. It falls down to the sea with a sheer 600m rock face and at its feet a skeleton from prehistoric times was found in a cave. L'homme de l'Orméa below the cradle of the Alps – a fine beginning.

New horizon: the path to the cradle of the Alps with Roc d'Orméa.

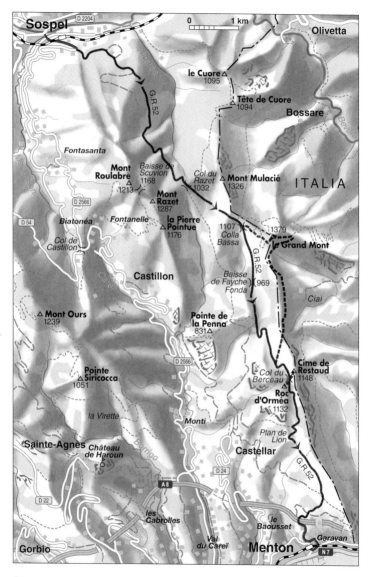

Sospel

D 2204

Olivetta

0   1 km

le Cuore △
1095

△ Tête de Cuore
1094

Bossare

G.R. 52

Fontasanta

Baisse de
Scuvion
1168

Col du
Razet
1032

△ Mont Mulacié
1326

ITALIA

Mont
Roulabre
△
1213

Mont
△ Razet
1287

1107
Colla
Bassa

1379

le Grand Mont

D 2566

Biatonéa

Fontanelle

la Pierre
△ Pointe
1176

G.R. 52

D 54

Col de
Castillon

Castillon

Baisse
de Fayche
Fonda

969

Ciai

△ Mont Ours
1239

Pointe de
la Penna
831△

Pointe
△ Siricocca
1051

D 2566

Col du
Berceau

Cime de
△ Restaud
1148

Roc
△ d'Orméa
1132

la Virette

Monti

Plan de
Lion

Sainte-Agnes

Château
de Haroun

Castellar

G.R. 52

D 24

A 8

D 22

les
Cabrolles

Val
du Careï

le
Baousset

Garavan

Gorbio

Menton

N 7

24

Beginning or end: twilight on the Orméa rocks. But where's the sea?

From the eastern edge of the village of **Sospel** where the link road from the station comes in you follow the D 2566 in the direction of the Col de Castillon until, after the first hairpin bend, the *GR 52* branches off right. Following a little road in places at the start, it goes onto a ridge (about 810m). The path dips a little behind this, crosses the eroded stream beds in the Fôret de l'Albaréa and eventually climbs up through this beech wood onto the **Col du Razet** (1032m).

On the left-hand path go past military and agricultural ruins and terraced slopes to the **Colla Bassa** (1107m). The *GR 52* goes along a dusty little access road to the **Baisse de Fayche Fonda** (969m) east of the conspicuous tower and then more steeply down to a fork at P. 838m. Follow the little road left into the first hairpin bend where the footpath branches off. It leads over terraced slopes and past the ruins of Vieux Castellar up to the **Col du Berceau** (about 1085m). Continue west along tracks up to the rocky summit of **Roc d'Orméa**.

Return to the col of the cradle and perhaps even up to the Cime de Restaud (1148m). Then go southwards, steeply down through a gully, full of scree at the top, to the **Plan de Lion** and to the fork (about 710m) of the *GR 51* and 52. Return south along the *GR 52* as in Walk 4 down to **Menton-Garavan**.

2 Mont Razet, 1285m

Views into and from the hinterland of Menton

Col de Castillon – Baisse de Scuvion – Mont Razet – La Pierre Pointue – Col de Castillon

Locations: Sospel: compare Walk 1; Menton: compare Walk 3.

Starting point and destination: Col de Castillon (706m) on the D 2566 from Menton to Sospel; the old road goes over the pass and at the top through a tunnel. The 'Chemin de la Crotta' bus stop is at the north entrance for the bus from Menton Gare Routière to Sospel Gare SNCF [TAM 910].

Walking times: Ascent and descent 1½ hours.

Ascent: 580m.

Distance: 6km.

Grade: Sure-footedness; some waymarkings.

Best time of year: All year round.

Accommodation: In Sospel: compare Walk 1; in Menton: compare Walk 4.

Alternative: A 5 hour round walk from Sospel (348m): ascent via L'Ibac and Piastrisse towards the Col de Castillon, descent from the gap by the Pierre Pointue over the Col du Razet and the GR 52 (as in Walk 1).

Places of Interest: Numerous lilies in the area, the snow on the highest summits of the Alpes Maritimes in the distance and Corsica on a clear day.

Map: TOP 25: Vallée de la Bévéra (3741 ET).

Adjoining walk: 1.

Ruins of a quite different nature: in the gaps north and south of Mont Razet there are hidden bunkers. Les blockhaus, the French expression for concrete command posts, were erected in defence against Mussolini's army. At this point, Italy is only a machine gun volley away from France. In June 1940 bloody battles took place between both countries. Castillon itself was almost totally destroyed after the landing of the Allies in 1944. The houses of Fontanelle on the west flank of Mont Razet served a peaceful purpose. The terraced slopes show evidence of former agriculture. A spring ensured the cultivation of the steep sunny slopes. And then below the village of Castillon the semi-circular Viaduc du Ciaramel springs into view, a relic of the narrow-gauge railway from Menton to Sospel.

From the north entrance of the vertex tunnel on the **Col de Castillon** go along a narrow tarmac road round two hairpin bends up to a car park above the tunnel. Continue another good 500m northwards along a little tarmac road until the narrow path turns off left (yellow and blue markings). Mostly in

Ruins of the alpine Maginot line: narrow pass at Pierre Pointue.

shade, it goes upwards along the north side of a ridge, winds along the partly rocky west flank of Mont Roulabre and eventually goes across the south flank of this into the **Baisse de Scuvion** (1158m). There are now 2 alternatives:

1) NW ridge: ascend the left of the two tracks going up from the pass. It is marked blue, goes up the west flank of the NW ridge, but then turns right below the N summit of Mont Razet (1287m, pole) and also below the south summit (1285m) onto the uppermost south ridge. You can also finish the ascent over the NW ridge.

2) West flank: from the Baisse de Scuvion return on the ascent path to the first zigzag and with little loss of height go across the steep west slope of Mont Razet into the gap at the Pierre Pointue. Immediately after the first bunker go up left on a track to the south ridge and keep on this track along the ridge to the south summit of **Mont Razet**.

Go back over the south ridge to the **Pierre Pointue** (1176m) and descend on a stony, fairly steep and unmarked path on the south west flank (the correct route is indicated with signposts).The path levels out below the rocks and goes across the slope, past a spring and the deserted settlement of Fontanelle. It eventually leads into the little road which brings you back to the **Col de Castillon**.

3 Cime de Baudon, 1264m

From eyrie to eyrie, from Saracen castle to panoramic peak

Sainte-Agnès – Château de Haroun – Cime de Baudon – Col de la Madone de Gorbio – Gorbio

Location: Menton (0m) on the train line Nice – Ventimiglia – Genua.

Starting point: Sainte-Agnès (670m) above Menton; bus from the Gare Routière which is northeast of the station on Avenue Sospel [TAM 902].

Destination: Gorbio (376m) above Menton; bus to the Gare Routière [TAM 901]. Autocars Breuleux travel daily to both places, tel: 04 93 35 73 51.

Walking times: Detour to the castle ruins in Ste-Agnès ½ hour, Ste-Agnès – Cime de Baudon 2½ hours, Cime de Baudon – Gorbio 1½ hours. Total time 4½ hours.

Ascent: 760m, descent 1040m.

Distance: 8km.

Grade: Sure-footedness needed at the Château de Haroun in Ste-Agnès and at the Cime de Baudon; blue waymarkings for most of the way.

Best time of year: All year round.

Refreshments and accommodation: In Ste-Agnès: compare Walk 4. In Gorbio: Auberge du Village, tel: 04 93 35 87 83; Camping La Giandolla with very beautiful sites, but the sanitary installations are not quite up to standard.

Alternative: from Gorbio on the GR 51 (compare Walk 5) in 1½ hours. Return to Ste-Agnès (390m ascent and 100m descent, 3km). Or do the walk in the other direction.

Places of Interest: The panorama.

Map: TOP 25: Nice – Menton (3742 OT).

Tip: Fort Ste-Agnès: a fortress built on the rocks of Ste-Agnès between 1932-38 to reinforce the Maginot Line, and whose artillery is aimed at Italy, open Sat. and Sun. 14.30-17.30; information from the Mairie, tel: 04 93 35 84 58.

Adjoining walks: 4, 5.

This summit walk in the Haut Pays Mentonnais has 4 particular highlights. Two wonderful viewing points, the Cime de Baudon and the castle ruins of the Saracen Prince 'Haroun el Rachid' (the noble Haroun) on the rock. Here,

To steep for beach walkers: Cime de Baudon seen from the Cime de Bausson.

on its west flank, the medieval village of St. Agnès sits like an eyrie. Two mountain villages with their houses built closely together and the picturesque tiny streets in between – these are typical villages perchés high up in the Côte d'Azur hinterland. And St. Agnès and Gorbio do not consist exclusively of craft shops and restaurants – people live there too.

Follow the signs to the Château through the village of **Ste Agnès**. Go past the cemetery along a stabilised path up to a shoulder with a cross on the south side of the rock of the village (easy up to here). Continue up to the ruined castle and finally along tracks to the **Château de Haroun** (766m), where you will find a panorama guide. Go back to the village and go down Promenade Saint-Sébastion to the square of the same name (602m) where there's a fork in the road and a bus stop. Go westwards past a spring (and left at the turn-off to the Col de Bausson). Go northwestwards on the flank of the Cime de Bausson to the Pas de Piastre and steeply up to a col west of the Cime de Bausson. Two paths join from the right along the way. Below the eastern ridge of the Cime de Baudon the path ascends through the dense wood on the north flank and eventually comes to the flat summit of the **Cime de Baudon**. Descend over the west ridge to a col. The path zigzags down fairly steeply on the south flank and goes along a ridge to the **Col de la Madone de Gorbio** (925m). Cross over the road and keeping left at the next fork, descend the path through the Ravin de Rank to **Gorbio**. As you approach the village you are walking sometimes along little concrete roads.

4 From Menton to Sainte-Agnès

First stage of the *GR 51* 'Balcons de la Côte d'Azur' – quite a path!

Menton-Garavan – Plan de Lion – Castellar – Monti – Ste-Agnès

Starting point: Menton-Garavan (0m); first or last train station on French soil for the Nice – Ventimiglia line; only local trains stop here.

Destination: Ste-Agnès (670m); compare Walk 3.

Walking times: Menton-Garavan – Castellar 2½ hours, Castellar – Ste-Agnès 3 hours. Total time 5½ hours.

Ascent: 1280m, descent 620m.

Distance: 15km.

Grade: Technically easy; red and white waymarkings throughout.

Best time of year: all year round; (too) hot in summer. The lemon festival takes place in February in Menton.

Refreshments and accommodation: In Menton: Auberge de Jeunesse, tel: 04 93 89 23 64, fax: 04 93 35 93 07. In Castellar: Hôtel des Alpes, tel: 04 93 35 82 83. In Ste-Agnès: Hôtel Saint-Yves, tel: 04 93 35 91 45.

Alternative: From the col at P. 748m there's a short but worthwhile detour on a path to the French-Italian border. The sign 'Sentier Européen' indicates that the *GR 51* is actually the continuation of the Via Alta dei Monti Liguri; beautiful views of the Riviera. A bus goes from Menton Gare Routière to Castellar [TAM 903].

Places of Interest: A brilliantly laid path in some sections, through green countryside with cypress and olive trees, lemon and mandarin trees.

Map: TOP 25: Nice – Menton (3742 OT).

Tip: Grocery shops in Ste-Agnès open daily and Sundays too.

Adjoining walks: 1, 3, 5, 45.

Per pedes behind the coast: November ambiance between Castellar and Monti.

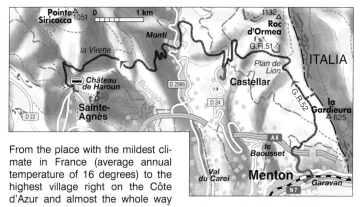

From the place with the mildest climate in France (average annual temperature of 16 degrees) to the highest village right on the Côte d'Azur and almost the whole way along old link paths: the long distance path, a good 500km, with the promising name 'Belvedere of the azure-blue coast' could not begin in a sunnier spot.

From **Menton-Garavan** train station do down the road towards Italy and left under the railway. On the left you will see the first red and white waymarking, the beginning of the *GR 51* and *52*. Go up small alleyways and steps through the exclusive residential district of Menton-Garavan. Unfortunately there are a few stretches on the road, near the Jardin des Colombières, for example, and the underpass for the very busy 'La Provençale'. Soon afterwards the GR leaves the last access road and climbs steeply up the predominantly wooded and sunny slopes to a col at P. 748.

Then you come to the Plan de Leuze, the **Plan de Lion** and the fork of the *GRs 51* and *52*. Descend westwards, first on a path, then on little gravel and tarmac roads to **Castellar** (342m). It's worth making the short ascent into the village (371m) to get ice creams and spring water. Return to the path by the chapel at the northern foot of the hill. The old link path descends across side valleys and through some properties, and eventually reaches the bridge (about 150m) over the Careï. With a few ups and downs you go over a tributary into the hamlet of **Monti** on the road from Menton to Sospel.

Go past the church and up to a shoulder on broad paths. The *GR of the Balcons de la Côte d'Azur* follows the old link path which crosses the steep slopes of two side valleys, goes through the ruins of La Virette and bridges the Borrigo river below the rock faces. Proceed through deserted agricultural buildings and terraces to reach the crossroads below the village and on a paved path you come straight to the main narrow street of **Ste-Agnès**.

5 From Sainte Agnès via La Turbie to Èze-Bord-de-Mer

The Grande Corniche for walkers high above the principality of Monaco

St. Agnès – Gorbio – Col de la Coupière – Col du Mont-Gros – Radio Monte-Carlo – Col de Guerre – Mont de la Bataille – La Turbie – Cime de la Forna – Èze – Èze-Bord-de-Mer

Starting point: Ste-Agnès (670m); compare Walk 3.

Destination: Èze-Bord-de-Mer (20m); local train or bus [Rapides Côte d'Azur] direction Nice or Monaco and Menten.

Walking times: Ste-Agnès – Gorbio 1 hour, Gorbio – col at Mont Gros 1¼ hours, Mont Gros – Col de Guerre 1¼ hours, Col de Guerre – Mont de la Bataille – La Turbie ¾ hours, La Turbie – Cime de la Forna – viewing platform 1 hour, descent to Èze-Bord-de-Mer 1¼ hours. Total time 6½ hours.

Ascent: 800m, descent 1450m.

Distance: 18 km (11 km to La Turbie).

Grade: Easy but long, on the white and red GR 51 as far as Col de Guerre GR 51; then only marked in places.

Best time of year: All year round; (too) hot in summer.

Refreshments and accommodation: In Ste-Agnès: compare Walk 4. Gorbio: compare Walk 3. La Turbie: Hôtel Cesarée, tel: 04 93 41 16 08; the wonderfully rustic Gîte d'étape Ferme de la Gorra north of and below the Col de Guerre on the GR 51, tel: 04 93 41 15 58.

Alternative: Start in or only go as far as La Turbie. Bus Monaco – La Turbie with Nice Excursions (only Mon. to Sat. 12.00; tel: 04 93 14 10 50). Descent from La Turbie to Monaco: from the Hotel Cesarée go down along the *Chemin romain vers Sotto Baou* to the turn-off. Go right onto the gravel path which turns into on old paved mule path. Cross the Chemin des Starras (small road). Descend a footpath through terraced olive groves with a few houses to the N7 (at the Restaurant Le Pont). Cross the road and descend a path down some steps (Chemin Grima) to Monaco. Where the path ends keep going right on roads and down steps to the Chemin de la Turbie. At the end of this keep right, along the road to Monaco station. 1 hour.

Places of Interest: view down to the sea of houses in Monte Carlo and Monaco and of the Italian and French Riviera.

Map: TOP 25: Nice – Menton (3742 OT).

Tip: Visit the Trophée des Alpes in La Turbie; open 9-12.00 and 14-17.00.

Adjoining walks: 3, 4, 6, 45.

This ridge walk high above the Grande Corniche is not completely free of cars, but the air is noticeably better than on the highest coastal road built by Napoleon between Menton and Nice which follows the ancient Via Julia Augusta in places. In La Turbie the Roman roads, the Renault drivers and the hikers all converge. This is where you will find the Trophée des Alpes, the almost 50m high monument in honour of Emperor Augustus, with the names of the 44 defeated tribes carved into its plinth. I wonder if the tower blocks of Monaco with the nameplates of tax dodgers will also last 2000 years?

Descend through the village of **Ste-Agnès** to the Promenade St. Sébastien from which the GR 51 of the *Balcons de la Côte d'Azur* turns off left (sign). It descends through a valley to the D 22. Go up along this road. Just before the

Peace and quiet instead of roulette: Ste-Agnès, the highest coastal village.

hairpin bend the path turns off left to **Gorbio** (376m).
Leave Gorbio on the upper road going south (not on the D 50). The *GR* goes round the north of the cemetery on paths, but this is not necessary since it meets the road to the **Col de la Coupière** again a bit further up. Go southwards on a roadway on the steep flank high above the Baie de Roque-brune towards Mont Gros. Here the partly replaced path leaves the roadway. The *GR* circumnavigates Mont Gros on the south side in a spectacular fashion, yet reaches a climax in a distinctive climb. But you can leave this turn-off on your left and ascend a new path on the east side. Both routes lead to a col northwest of Mont Gros (favourite jumping off point for paragliders). Go up a little road onto a hill (680m) and down to the **Col du Mont Gros** (about 660m).
Follow a tarmac road to the entrance for the **Radio Monte-Carlo** station (P. 785m). Soon afterwards the road descends to the Col de Guerre which walkers can reach on a direct path (don't miss the marked turn-off!). From the **Col de Guerre** (550m) go a short way westwards on a road until a path turns off left to **Mont de la Bataille** (620m). From here descend comfortably down to **La Turbie** (479m) along a mule track.
Continue along the Grande Corniche D 2564 in the direction of Col d'Èze until 300m after the turn-off for the motorway slip road a cul-de-sac branches off right to some houses (yellow waymarkings). You reach the Parc Forestier Départemental de la Grande Corniche and continue up a path onto the hill where it leads into a little gravel road. This leads to the **Cime de la Forna** (621m). The summit cairn can be found a few metres above the little road.

Flowers instead of concrete: view from Mont Gros of Monte Carlo and Monaco.

Continue along this road, which originally used to serve the military, as far as the point where a path branches off right by the second tunnel and zigzags up to the ridge. You soon reach the information board on a low stone turret (about 660m).

Descend westwards on part of the *Sentier botanique* down to a car park at the **Maison de la Nature** below the Fort de la Rivière (696m). There you will find a sign to Èze. Zigzag down on a narrow path, then go right and at the fork, left. The path goes across a little concrete road which joins the Grande Corniche. Go eastwards for a few metres until you find a grassy path on the left which leads to a very steep little concrete road. Take the right fork and descend to the Corniche Moyenne which leads up to the **Èze-Village** cross-roads (356m).

Descend on the path described in Walk 6 to **Èze-Bord-de-Mer** where you can dive straight into the Mer d'Èze.

6 Èze and Mont Bastide, 560m

Almost vertical walk to a tourist village and a stone wall

Èze-Bord-de-Mer – Sentier Nietzsche – Èze-Village – Mont Bastide – Èze-Bord-de-Mer

Starting point and destination: Èze-Bord-de-Mer (20m); compare Walk 5. In summer there's a bus connection between Èze coast, village and pass.

Walking times: Èze-Bord-de-Mer – Èze-Village 1¼ hours, village – Mont Bastide ¾ hours, descent to the sea 1 hour. Total time 3 hours.

Ascent: 610m.

Distance: 5km.

Grade: Some sure-footedness and fitness required. Marked paths.

Best time of year: All year round. Best time at sunrise or sunset on Mont Bastide.

Refreshments: Numerous (expensive) restaurants in Èze.

Accommodation: In Èze itself only luxury hotels. L'Hermitage du Col d'Èze, tel: 04 93 41 00 68. Auberge Eric Rivot in Èze-Bord-de-Mer, tel: 04 93 01 51 46. Camping Les Romarins on the Grande Corniche west of Col d'Èze, tel: 04 93 01 81 64.

Alternative: From Eze station by local train to Cap d'Ail and then take the *sentier littoral* to the Plage Marquet; 30 min.

Places of Interest: Les trois Corniches, the three coast roads: not even Cabriolet owners will get better views.

Map: TOP 25: Nice – Menton (3742 OT).

Tip: Take swimwear for Èze bay. The Jardin exotique in Èze, entrance fee, is open from June – mid-October from 8-20.00 and mid-October – May from 9-17.00.

Adjoining walks: 5, 45.

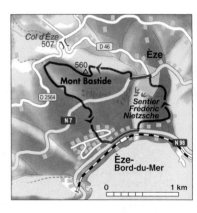

Walk into the village of Èze where well-heeled residents and tourists drive to in the evenings in their Ferraris and Porsches. The village perché was founded by the Phoenicians and dedicated to the goddess Isis. The castle, originally built as a siege castle, is now given over to tourism, full to overflowing with smart shops, totally overrun by visitors, but still has a delightful position above the idyllic coast. To enjoy the best view of Èze climb up to Mont Bastide. Here on top of this little known rock you can sit alone amongst the ruins of a castle from pre-Roman times and freely admire the view.

From the station in **Èze-Bord-de-Mer** go a few steps up onto the Corniche Inférieure. Go along this for a few minutes towards Monaco until on the left, the red marked *Sentier Frédéric Nietzsche* turns off in the direction of Èze-village. It climbs up between villas and then steep rocks over to the Vallon du

Duc and through this valley straight into the old part of **Èze-village** (427m). Walk down through the village to the crossroads (356m) in the new part. Go along the Corniche Moyenne on the right hand side over a viaduct. The *Sentier du Mont Bastide* begins at the end of this. After a loop at the start, it leads up above the road (somewhat exposed, but with a delightful view of Èze) mostly on the far side of the mountain (easily climbed) and finally over the east ridge to the summit of **Mont Bastide**.

Descend on a good path to the uppermost coast road, the Grande Corniche, which you reach to the west of the Col d'Eze. The blue marked *Chemin de Caricart* begins (signpost) before you come to the road. Descend through a valley on a path to the Corniche Moyenne. Cross over this and descend on the blue marked *Chemin de Savaric* straight to the station of **Èze-Bord-de-Mer**. The path at the end is concrete and steep. Be careful not to miss the steps on the left after the first houses.

Superb address: Èze, the most expensive of all the village perchés on the elegant coast. If you want to stay overnight here, do not come on foot.

Cap Ferrat peninsula

On the *sentier touristique* around the garden of Eden

Beaulieu-sur-Mer – Saint-Jean-Cap-Ferrat – Point de St-Hospice – Cap Ferrat – Villa et Jardins Ephrussi de Rothschild – Beaulieu-sur-Mer

Starting point and destination: Beaulieu-sur-Mer (0m) on the train and bus route Nice – Menton. Bus from Nice Gare Routière to St-Jean-Cap-Ferrat harbour [TAM 111; except Sun. and Bank Holidays; tel: 04 93 55 24 00].

Walking time: 3-4 hours.

Ascent: About 100m.

Distance: 13 km (round walk from St-Jean-Cap-Ferrat 3 km shorter).

Grade: Trainers; hardly any waymarkings, but easy to find your way.

Best time of year: All year round.

Refreshments: Various restaurants; Paloma Beach, Le Grand Bleu on the Plage de Passable and Villa Ephrussi de Rothschild.

Accommodation: In St-Jean-Cap-Ferrat: Bagatelle, tel: 04 93 01 32 86, fax: 04 93 01 41 00; Clair Logis, tel: 04 93 76 04 57, fax: 04 93 76 11 85; Bastide, tel: 04 93 76 06 78, fax: 04 93 76 19 10.

Places of Interest: Luxury villas (most of them from the outside only). The seven gardens of Villa Ephrussi de Rothschild.

Map: TOP 25: Nice – Menton (3742 OT).

Tip: Villa Kérylos: open all year, only afternoons in winter, tel: 04 93 01 01 44. Musée Fondation Ephrussi de Rotschild (villa and gardens), mid-Feb until end Oct. daily 10-18.00, otherwise 14-18.00, tel: 04 93 01 33 09. More information about the villas

and their occupiers can be found in the illustrated book by S. Johnston and R. Schezen *The Villas of the Riviera*.

The peninsular of the totally rich: the finest villas, trees and flowers, and also the finest location. From where else could you get on outside view, so to speak, of the Côte d'Azur than from places on the Presqu'Île du Cap Ferrat – and of course from the fantastic yachts which tend to moor in the harbour of Saint-Jean-Cap-Ferrat fishing village. Cap Ferrat is a paradise for those who have a residence there and for those others who walk along by the sea on the *sentier touristique*.

From **Beaulieu-sur-Mer** station go down to the main road, Boulevard Maréchal Leclerc. Shortly after the railway underpass turn right into the little

Coastline of the rich: cliff path on the west side of Cap Ferat. The sun doesn't cost anything.

used Rue du Lieutenant Colonelli leading to the yacht harbour which lies diagonally opposite the casino. You soon reach the entrance to the **Villa Kérylos** on the left hand side. Now keep walking along the promenade as far as **St-Jean-Cap-Ferrat**. Go down left as soon as possible to the beach and the harbour. Before the path goes out left onto the harbour mole go up right to the road and follow it as far as the Plage Paloma. Go down the steps to the restaurant and walk through. Go round the **Pointe de St-Hospice** on a concrete shore path. On the way there's a turn-off to the Chapelle St-Hospice. Finally go along a forest path which leads to a road. Go along this to Les Fossettes and Les Fosse bays. At the crossroads keep to the left. Go straight on at the barrier. Continue along the shore (on concrete at first) round **Cap Ferrat**. The shore path on the west side of the peninsula stops at the big apartment block 'Le Lido'. Go down behind this to the Plage de Passable. Go up some steps, continue straight on along a footpath, then to a crossroads. You reach the main road (with Passable bus stop) along the *Chemin de Passable*. Go northwards along the road to the entrance to the **Fondation Ephrussi de Rothschild** (60m). After visiting the villa and gardens go back to the main road, immediately keep sharp left and then turn right into the Allée de Tilleul. Go down to the sea and continue along the promenade northwards to **Beaulieu-sur-Mer** or southwards to **Saint-Jean-Cap-Ferrat**.

8 Cime de Roccassièra, 1501m

A village, a village ruin, a summit and a hotel: unforgettable

Coaraze – Col St-Michel – Ruines de Rocca-Sparvièra – Cime de Roccassièra – Coaraze

Starting point and destination: Coaraze (640 m) on the D 15 in the Contes valley north of Nice. Bus from Nice Gare Routière [TAM 303]; good bus service to Contes from where people from the Auberge du Soleil will come to pick you up (a night in this hotel is recommended).

Walking times: Ascent 3½ hours, descent 2½ hours. Total time 6 hours.

Ascent: About 900m.

Distance: 16km.

Grade: Sometimes narrow paths which demand sure-footedness. Blue and yellow or just yellow waymarkings.

Best time of year: May to October.

Refreshments and accommodation: Auberge du Soleil in Coaraze, tel: 04 93 79 08 11, fax: 04 93 79 37 79.

Alternative: From the summit in 3 hours via the Lobe, Porte and St-Roch passes, mostly on the *GR 510*, to Lucéram (604m); Hôtel La Méditerranée, tel: 04 93 79 51 93. Bus to Nice [TAM 350, 360].

Places of Interest: The winding alleyways and the sun dials in Coaraze. The ruins of houses and the terraced slopes of Rocca-Sparvièra. The view of the Pays niçois from the second highest summit in this guide. The view from the lavender room of the 'Auberge du Soleil'.

Map: TOP 25: Vallée de la Bévéra (3741 ET).

Tip: The small useful guide with 30 walks from Coaraze is available from the tourist office. Guided walks with the organisation A.P.A.C.H.E.S, tel: 04 93 79 34 54.

Adjoining walk: 9; nicest to climb onto Mont Férion (1412m) and then walk along its 7 km long south ridge to the Col de Châteauneuf-de-Contes (description in the Coaraze guide).

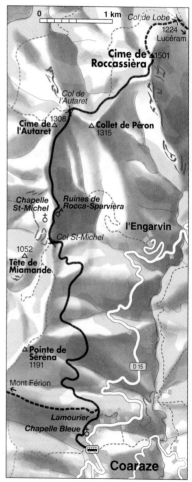

Coaraze, which is tucked away almost at the back of the valley of the Paillon de Contes, is one of the most beautiful villages in France. That in itself is a reason to travel there by bus from Nice. But awaiting you is this walk on ancient paths over steep slopes full of gorse and pine trees to the Cime de Roccassièra above the Gorges de Vésubie. About half way up to the top on a spur in the middle of a barren landscape are the ruins of a village in which 500 people once lived (as many as in Coaraze today). An earthquake in 1618 put on end to this life in the mountains. The view of the coast, however much it is overdeveloped, is still captivating.

From the village square in **Coaraze** go westwards left past 'Les Arts' bar and follow the little road to the chapel. Turn left just afterwards onto a gravel road which leads up to a rib.

More than a path: it links magical places in the highlands of Nice.

Now begins the long climb up to the Col St-Michel across a steep east-facing flank which is divided by ridges and gullies and sparsely covered in trees. The path is narrow and in places exposed, especially between the first and second gully and also before the Col St-Michel. It descends for a short way at the start and also just before the pass.

From the **Col St-Michel** (about 960m) go westwards below a rock tower and zigzag across the precipitous flank to the Chapelle St-Michel. Go through the **ruins of Rocca-Sparvièra** and continue northwards gradually ascending above the terraced slopes, then across the terraces themselves to the plateau and the Col de l'Autaret.

The path to the Cime de Roccassièra branches off right, crosses a wooded slope and follows a ridge, partly wooded, to the summit. The path zigzags steeply upwards. A few metres below the summit ridge a track goes off right to the south summit (1494m) from which you have a better view over to Coaraze. Return to the main path and over a few boulders, where it's necessary to use your hands, as far as the end of the summit ridge of the **Cime de Roccassièra** (also called Rocca Serra). Descend the same way you came up.

9 Mont Macaron, 806m

Sleeping Beauty 9km inland from the heavenly bay of Nice

Tourrette-Levens – col and ruins of Châteauneuf – Mont Macaron – Col de Bordinas – Tourrette-Levens

Starting point and destination: Tourrette-Levens (about 400m) on the D 19 north of Nice; to be precise, the new suburb of Le Plan (about 360m) at the turn-off of the D 719 to Aspremont. Bus from Nice Gare Routière [TAM 310: Nice – Tourrette-Levens – Levens, tel: 04 93 89 47 14; TAM 320: Nice – Tourrette-Levens – Châteauneuf-de-Contes, tel: 04 93 91 09 90].

Walking times: Tourrette-Levens – Ruines de Châteauneuf 1¼ hours, ruins – Mont Macaron ¾ hour, summit – Col de Bordinas ½ hour, return to the village 1 hour. Total time 3½ hours.

Ascent: 660m.

Distance: 11km.

Grade: Marked throughout with yellow arrows and dots and in places with red and white waymarkings (*GR 51*).

Best time of year: All year round.

Refreshments: In Tourrette-Levens.

Accommodation: In Tourrette-Levens. In Aspremont: compare Walk 10.

Alternative: Start in Cantaron (99m) on the train line Nice-Sospel and on the bus route to Contes (compare Walk 8); you reach the Col de Bordinas (475m) in 1 hour on the *GR 51*; compare Walk 45.

Places of Interest: The fairytale ruins of Châteauneuf: a mountain village built on a Roman fort (Castellum Novum), half in ruins, almost completely overgrown.

Map: TOP 25: Nice – Menton (3742 OT).

Tip: Butterfly museum in the castle in the old part of Tourrette-Levens, open in summer 14-19.00, winter 14-17.00.

Adjoining walks: 10: from Tourrette-Levens on the *GR 51* to Aspremont; 45 min. to the turn-off of the path to Mont Chauve. 45.

Mont Macaron is one of the few summits on the coast by Nice which has not been developed. There's no fortress, no antenna, no village – just a circle of ruined walls. The round walk is the same: there are hardly any tarmac roads, instead there are times when you are walking totally surrounded by greenery – no villas, no roads, only gorse and pines, and on the ascent to Tourrette-Levens olive and fig trees on terraced slopes through which the paved mule track runs. Even more picturesque is the *chemin pavé* from the Rio Sec up to the Col de Châteauneuf.

Reclaiming the old out of new growth: the medieval ruins of Castellum Novum.

From the crossroads in **Le Plan** (bus stop on the road to Aspremont) go along the D 19 in the direction of Levens and after the second house on the right descend the path, still concrete at first, to the Rio Sec. The paved mule track through the pine wood begins after the bridge (333m), keeps getting lost in the exclusive residential area of La Vignasse and finally, before the **Col de Châteauneuf** (626m), disappears in approach roads to houses. Go southwards from the pass along the path above the road to the eastern end of the **ruins of Châteauneuf**. Go left and along trodden paths through a deserted village (750m). Return and continue straight ahead to the Chapelle St-Joseph (709m). Now on the path (not on the little road) go along the north ridge to **Mont Macaron**, at first on the right of the ridge, then on the left and lastly on the right for quite a way. When the path reaches the top of the ridge again, climb the path straight to the summit.

Go along the ridge to the south summit (787m), descend southwards to a col and zigzag down across south-facing slopes to the **Col de Bordinas** or Baisse de Rougier (475m). Here you meet the *GR 51*. Follow a road through a wood for a little way then descend on a path into a valley and at first on the left hand side, later on the right hand side, you come to the hamlet of Tra la Torre (254m). After the bridge across the Rio Sec go up a *chemin pavé* to **Tourrette-Levens**. At the entrance to the village go straight on through the narrow street to the church or left to a car park and to the castle (443m). Return finally on the village road to **Le Plan**.

10 Mont Chauve d'Aspremont, 853m

Above the roofs of Nice

Aspremont – Baisse de Guigo – Mont Chauve d'Aspremont – Aspremont

Starting point and destination: Aspremont (499m) north of Nice at the crossroads of the D 14, D 414 and D 719; bus from Nice Gare Routière [Rapides Côte d'Azur; TAM 104, tel: 04 93 55 24 00].

Walking times: Ascent 1½ hours, descent 1 hour. Total time 2½ hours.

Ascent: Just under 400m.

Distance: 7km.

Grade: You will need some courage for the moats in the fortress. The path over the eastern slope is not well-trodden; marked yellow and, in places, red and white (*GR 51* and *5*).

Best time of year: All year round.

Refreshments and accommodation: Hostellerie d'Aspremont, tel: 04 93 08 00 05; Hôtel le Saint Jean, tel: 04 93 08 00 66.

Alternative: You can also go as far as a turn-off south of the Baisse de Guigo and then come to the eastern slope through a dark tunnel.

And: descend the last part of the *GR 5* which is part of the long distance path Amsterdam-Nice, down into the town to the Place Alexandre Médecin and carry straight on to the station; 8km, 2 hours.

Places of Interest: The most important town on the Côte d'Azur from a bird's eye view.

Map: TOP 25: Nice – Menton (3472 OT).

Tip: Mont Chauve de Tourrette is not accessible; the fortress is used by French authorities as a shooting range.

Adjoining walks: 9, 45.

The walk on and around Mont Chauve (chauve = bald) is a good introduction to walking in the mountains of the Côte d'Azur – the kind of paths, the waymarkings, the vegetation, the views, the terraced slopes (called restanques), the empty fields, the military constructions.

From the crossroads in **Aspremont** you go a short way along the road in the direction of Nice. After passing the entrance to the car park and the bus stop the red and white marked *GR 51* and *GR 5* turn off right onto the *Chemin de la Vallière*.

Descend to a hairpin bend on the road to Nice. Go eastwards on little roads and a path. The *GR 5* branches off right (you return on this). Continue along the *GR 51* as far as the col where you leave it to go along a track to a farm

Walking in the moat: you suddenly plunge into the moat from the fort above.

house. The path goes up right, past the farm house, and through a light wood. Before the spacious **Baisse de Guigo** the yellow marked route turns off onto a narrow path. It runs diagonally upwards into a little hidden valley on the eastern slope of Mont Chauve d'Aspremont. The path, still marked yellow, ascends across the eastern slope up onto the north ridge. Go along the ridge to the fortress, the dimensions and moats of which are only visible at the last moment. Keep to the left until you can go down some steps into the outer moat. Walk along to the front and go up some steps to the entrance gate and up some more to the viewing terrace on the outer ring of the fortress of **Mont Chauve d'Aspremont**.

Descend the approach road. Before it leads over to the Baisse de Guigo you turn sharp right. Continue westwards on a broad path to the *GR 5*. It leads over the western flank of Mont Chauve, past ruins of agricultural buildings, back to the ascent route from **Aspremont**.

Haut Pays Grassois: stony waves

'The Gorges du Loup has an amazing landscape – rocks, ravines, waterfalls hanging like broad silver falls before plunging free to thunder down and spread into the valley.' What a pleasure it is to be listening to nature and reading culture at the same time. Erika and Klaus Mann called their idiosyncratic guide from 1931 to the Côte d'Azur *The book of the Riviera*. They made their big trip into the hinterland of Cannes by car. You, on the other hand, are on foot and can follow up their description of the Gorge du Loup with more leisure. 'Up there, at the highest point, lies Gourdon, the summit of the trip in every sense of the word. It is a strikingly wild landscape; the enormous grey rocks inflected with red and yellow are alone between the deep blue sky and the black shadowed chasms'.

The mountain village of Gourdon (Walk 15) lies at the convergence of highland and lowland. At the back there's the barrenness of the highlands of the perfume producing town of Grasse, and at the front the lush hilly countryside around the film capital of Cannes – a heavily built-up area alien to hikers. The Gorge du Loup looks as if it's been cut with a knife in the mountain range which it divides, the Haut Pays Grassois and the Haut Pays Vençois. The four summits of the highlands of Vence, the Baous, rise up like enormous ships' keels above the town of Vence and its neighbouring villages which have nearly all become famous for the homes of artists. The four cornerstones accessible on walks, the Baous of St-Jeannet and de la Gaude (Walk 11) as well as the Baous des Blancs and des Noirs above Vence, are part of the limestone mountains between the rivers of Var and Siagne.

In these mountains there are high karstic plateaus which are divided by parallel mountain ranges which remind you of enormous waves frozen in time. Even in this wild place the rough undergrowth doesn't prevent you from finding a way out. If you go over the ridges and high plains you repeatedly come across the stone remains of mountain farms especially the little field houses.

You will notice the difference between two kinds of stone construction. The shepherds' houses and shelters were built square, with big cut cornerstones and walls of irregular smaller stones which are held together with mortar. These houses where the shepherds lived seasonally, were covered with canvas.

In contrast to these are the round constructions with dry stone walls, like igloos made out of limestone. These ancient domed constructions with thick foundation walls and a narrow opening are called 'trulli' in Apulien, 'bories' in Provence. A borie is a shelter for shepherds as well as for field workers and where they used to keep their tools. There is often a stone sheep pen near to these buildngs.

Both types of building can be found on the Col de la Femme Morte. The borie

En vogue: entrance to the borie at Ci-pières, artistic-looking evidence of the Côte d'Azur's former mountain agri-culture.

there is one of the most remarkable buildings in the hinterland of the Côte d'Azur and is only accessible by walking for several hours (Walk 16). At the southern foot of Montagne du Cheiron in an area of 25 sq. km. there are 400 pieces of stone archeology from a previous era when the villages were still self-reliant and there were no Leclerc, Casino, and Géant supermarkets, or whatever else you'd like to call them, down on the coast. The Circuit de Cipières (Walk 14) illustrates this kind of world in the Haut Pays Grassois.

Typical for the mountain chains in the pre-Alps of Grasse, as shown inland as well, is its east-west alignment, experienced at its best on the traverse of Montagne du Cheiron (1778m). On the north side of the highest peak in this guide (Walk 13) there are green meadows with grazing sheep and on the south side, the scars of ski slopes on the terraces no longer in use. Two ways of using the resources of a mountain – one aesthetically pleasing, the other not, one sustainable, the other not: one is the result of hard work in the sun on the southern flank erecting all these walls, called restanques, the other constructed with firebreaks and snow canons for a quick profit.

But in spite of this, it is fun to go skiing there and further south. 'Panorama unique – vue sur la Côte d'Azur' – this is the promise made on the board at the mountain station of the longest ski lift in the l'Audibergue skiing area. A few minutes walk up to the highest point (1642m) of this mountain in the Haut Pays Grassois and you have only hills ahead and then the sea, 27km in the distance. The first (or last) limestone wave of the alpine arc. L'Audibergue, the southernmost skiing area of the Alps, lies directly above the Route Napoléon, the most famous road in France next to the Champs-Elysées. At the point where the Route Napoléon is best maintained, head up into the mountains (Walk 17).

11 Baou de Saint-Jeannet, 800m

An excellent mountain for climbing and walking

St-Jeannet – Baou de St-Jeannet – Château Le Castellet – St-Jeannet

Starting point and destination: St-Jeannet (425m) northeast of Vence. Various bus routes: from Nice Gare Routière via St-Laurent Gare SNCF (it's best to change here from the train to the bus) and La Gaude [Linie 222 bzw. 5], from St-Laurent-du-Var via Gattières [Linie 6], from Vence [Linie 13; all Var Mer buses, tel: 04 93 14 02 02].

Walking times: Ascent to the summit 1¼ hours, on to the farm 1 hour, descent 1¼ hours. Total time 3½ hours.

Ascent: About 500m.

Distance: 9.5km.

Grade: Sure-footedness; marked red and white (GR) and yellow; the path is not easy to find on the plateau.

Best time of year: All year round.

Refreshments: Le Chante Grill with Italian-Provençal cooking (closed Sun. evening and Mon.)

Accommodation: Gîte d'étape, tel: 04 93 24 87 11. Camping à la ferme D.G. Rasse on the Chemin des Sausses below the Baou de la Gaude, tel: 04 93 24 87 11: in the midst of vineyards, under olive trees and near cypress trees, with views of the Baous – nothing could be more beautiful.

Alternative: Baou de la Gaude (796m): quite a long walk if you start at the Camping à la Ferme, go 700m along the road to Gattièr, gain height on the *GR 51*, ascend a path northwestwards, go round La Colle (842m) on its west side and afterwards reach le Gros Chêne, one of the oldest oak trees in France (it stands just a short way below the path) and continue to the summit with the

Ligurian circular fortress; in order to enjoy the view you need to go right out onto the edge of the Baou de la Gaude. Descend eventually on the path into the Vallon de Parriau to the Route des Baou de St-Jeannet, 2 hours.

Places of interest: The Marina Baie de Anges between Cros-de-Cagnes and Antibes: four enormous complexes in the shape of pyramids with holiday apartments – the urban answer of 1970 to the four Baous in the Haut Pays Vençois.

Map: TOP 25: Vallée de l'Esteron (3643 ET).

Tip: Climbers will find everything in the SOeScalade/Marie Cord' shop in St-Jeannet (information, topos, equipment), tel: 04 93 24 46 15.

Adjoining walk: 45.

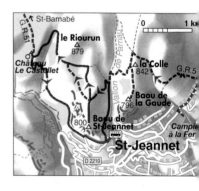

The Baou de St-Jeannet is not only the highest of the four Baous, but also the most beautiful and the most famous. With its 200m high rock faces it stands vertically above the pretty village of St-Jeannet. More than 200 routes have been put up by climbers. The mountain is the centre of climbing sport in Nice. A wine with character is cultivated at its foot and can be bought in the

A solitary climbing genius: chance meeting on the Baou de la Gaude.

village. It can give a special touch to a picnic at Le Castellet castle dating from 1309. This enormous ruin at the edge of the Haut Pays Vençois is one of the memorable buildings on the Côte d'Azur.

From the car park below go up to the old part of **St-Jeannet** village. Follow the signposts through the narrow streets to the Baou St-Jeannet and eventually turn into the *Chemin de Baou* along which the GR51 also runs. The good path climbs up through the Vallon de Parriau between Baou St-Jeannet and Baou de la Gaude. Still in the valley, at signpost 4, you leave the *GR 51* to the left and go up south of La Roque hill onto the summit ridge. Go south along a path which loses itself in the karstic landscape and along the ridge to the summit of the **Baou de St-Jeannet** (panorama guide). Return on the same path to signpost 5. Do not descend to the right, instead continue straight on over the undulating high plain as far as the *GR 51* (signpost 6). Two routes are possible, but at the fork 5 take the left one, an infrequently yellow-marked path which leads halfway through a hollow, comes to a borie hidden in a little wood and eventually reaches the *GR 51* going north over karstic terrain. Go along the *GR 51* to the west and through the Combe Maougaride to the Chàteau Le Castellet (not named on the IGN map). The *GR 51* turns off just before. Descend the yellow marked path into the valley of the Cagne and below the rock faces of the Baou de St-Jeannet return to the **St-Jeannet** village.

12 Pic de Cormettes, 1248m – Puy de Tourrettes, 1268m

The view of the sea, so near and yet so far

Tourrettes-sur-Loup – Pic de Courmettes – Puy de Tourrettes – St-Barnabé plateau and hamlet – Combe de Maigré – Tourrettes-sur-Loup

Starting point and destination: Tourrettes-sur-Loup (401m) on the D 2210 between Grasse and Vence. Bus from Grasse via Pont du Loup [TAM 510, 511].

Walking times: Ascent to the Pic de Gourmettes 3 hours, on to the Puy de Tourrettes ½ hour, descent to St-Barnabé 1½ hours, return to Tourrettes-sur-Loup 2¾ hours. Total time about 8 hours.

Ascent: 1000m.

Distance: 19km.

Grade: You should not go on this walk if you can't find your way through the alleyways of Tourrettes-sur-Loup old town and thereby miss the elegant boutiques. Difficult route-finding in the fog from Pic de Gourmettes to *GR 51*. Some waymarkings, but very varied (red and white, coloured spots, cairns).

Best time of year: All year round; (too) hot in summer.

Refreshments: Hostels in St-Barnabé; splendid village spring in Tourrettes-sur-Loup.

Accommodation: In Tourrettes-sur-Loup: Hôtel Les Belles Terrasses, tel: 01 93 59 30 03; Camping La Camassade, tel: 04 93 59 31 54. In St-Barnabé: Auberge St-Martin, always open, 6 places in a caravan, tel: 04 93 59 11 66. In Courmes: Auberge de Courmes, tel: 04 93 77 64 70. In Vence: Auberge de Seigneurs, tel: 04 93 58 04 24; Hôtel La Roserai, tel: 04 93 58 02 20; Camping Domaine de la Bergerie, tel: 04 93 58 09 36. In Le-Bar-sur-Loup: compare Walk 15.

Alternative: The summit walk from the pretty village of Courmes (623m). From Puy de Tourrettes descend via the north ridge straight to P. 973m above the Combe de Maigré. At signpost 69 take the path to Vence; you can also start from there.

Places of Interest: Ruins of the Saracen castle above Tourrettes-sur-Loup which was built from the same material as the nameless farming settlement on the northwest ridge of Puy de Tourettes.

Map: TOP 25: Cannes – Grasse (3643 ET).

Tip: From P. 948m, where you reach the *GR 51*, you can turn right to the agricultural buildings and after a derelict shepherds' hut go to the so-called 'village nègre', a collection of karstic formations reminiscent of African statues.

Adjoining walks: 13, 45.

The highlands of Vence have everything to offer – unique viewing points (from the Pic de Courmettes it's only 13km as the crow flies to the coast); varied paths from the little villa road above the GR of the *Balcons de la Côte d'Azur* to the stony paths through Mediterranean vegetation; the contrast between the tourist coastline and the remote karstic plain of St-Barnabé which is sometimes reminiscent of a desert and is still amazingly green; the descent to Le Malvan Rou ice cold stream through the sun-heated Combe de Maigré with its restanques and its terraces separated by dry stone walls.

The art of survival: dry stone walls in the dry Combe de Maigré.

From the main square in **Tourrettes-sur-Loup** go northwest to the Maison de la Presse and the Chapelle St-Jean. Continue along the Route de St-Jean, not missing a right hand bend, as far as the furthest villa called 'Le Paradis'. The path goes past it on the right and climbs up through thick gorse bushes and woods to a shoulder. It is narrow at first, but then broadens out as other paths join it. Finally, past a house with an antenna, you come to a little road where you turn left to a signpost indicating the path to the Pic de Courmettes which leads over the Domaine de Courmettes and the west ridge to the summit. However the following route is more direct: from the signpost take the broad path northwards over a grassy ridge to the ruin of the Jas de l'Eouvière. Now continue on mostly stony paths straight up to the top. Three metres before the path descends left you come to a cairn. It marks the start of stony paths which lead up through the wood still northwards as far as the edge of the wood (the route indicated on the topographical map is wrong). Now continue without paths to the northwest over karstic slopes (cairns) to

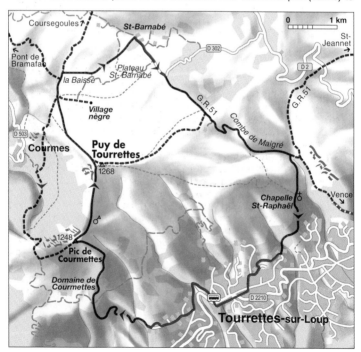

A change in the vegetation: a sea of ferns above Tourrettes-sur-Loup.

the trig point of the **Pic de Courmettes**. For most of the way go along a track to the right of the ridge, over to the **Puy de Tourrettes** where the highest point can be found somewhere on the grassy summit plateau. The col between both the summits is 1114m high. Go along a track across the broad northwest ridge (cairns) to ruins of farming buildings and along a path down to the GR51. Continue on this, being careful not to miss the turn-off at signpost 86 from **La Baisse**, across the St-Barnabé plateau to the settlement of **St-Barnabé** (967m).

You follow the approach road for a kilometre and then change onto a broad roadway which leads southeastwards into the **Combe de Maigré**. Go down through this hollow, first on a gravel path then on the narrow path on the left side of the valley. As you come out of the valley you leave the *GR 51* and descend to the right to signpost 69. Go once more right, over to the ice-cold Le Malvan Rau. Continue through (burnt) gorse landscape to the **Chapelle St-Raphaël** which you are not allowed to visit.

Afterwards go along a better path in the wood and up past a reservoir to the remains of a Saracen fortress. On a tarmac road through the exclusive residential quarter you reach the main road at the eastern edge of the village. At this point do not use the road bridge, instead go under it on a footpath. Return along a quiet little road to the Place de la Libération in **Tourrettes-sur-Loup**.

13 Montagne du Cheiron, 1778m

High point and ridge walk between the Alps and the Mediterranean

Coursegoules – La Croix de Verse – Jérusalem – Sommet des Crêtes – Cime du Cheiron – Gréolières

Starting point: Coursegoules (1035m) north of the Col de Vence on the D 2; no bus, but Tonio taxis from Gréolières, tel: 04 09 30 44 41 or 04 92 06 49 82.

Destination: Gréolières (839m) on the D 2 and D 79 almost at the very top of the course of the Loup. Infrequent bus service from Grasse [TAM 512; tel: 04 93 42 40 79].

Walking times: Coursegoules – Col de Coursegoules 1½ hours, pass – Jérusalem 2 hours, on to the Cime de Cheiron ½ hour, descent to Gréolières 2 hours. Total time 6 hours.

Ascent: A good 800m, descent a good 1000m.

Distance: 13km.

Grade: The east-west traverse, just under 8km long, is mostly without paths. Route-finding is therefore necessary although, in good visibility, you are unlikely to lose your way, added to which there are masts on all the summit ridge elevations. In fog the going is tough and it's best to keep to the edges of the enormous south flank. Make a very early start (heat, clouds, thunderstorms).

Best time of year: May to November. In winter and spring the north slopes of the Cheiron are overrun by the second most southern skiing playground in the Alps: Gréolières-les-Neiges.

Refreshments and accommodation: In Coursegoules: Auberge de l'Escaou, tel: 04 93 59 11 28, fax:: 04 93 59 13 70; campsite in the village. In Gréolières: Hôtel La Vieille Auberge, tel: 04 93 59 95 07.

Alternative: From Gréolières there are two footpaths back to Coursegoules; one goes across the treeless south flank in places, the other one through wooded valleys.

Places of Interest: In the north the Argentera (3287m), the highest summit of the Maritime Alps. In the west Provence. In the south Corsica and almost the whole of the Côte d'Azur. Alpine flora in the area as well.

Maps: TOP 25: Vallée de l'Estéron (3642 ET).

Tip: Guided walks as well as other adventurous trips with Préalpes 06 in Gréolières, tel: 04 93 59 98 81.

Adjoining walks: 14: 1 hour from Cipières to Gréolières. 12: 5km from signpost 86 on La Baisse as far as Coursegoules.

Montagne de Cheiron: a 1000 metre high and slightly concave wall diagonally above the valley of the Loup. The key points are Gréolières and Coursegoules, two of those compactly built villages in the mountains. From the village go along the old alpine path up to a pass and along the ridge to the eastern summit of Jérusalem. On the traverse to the western summit Cime de Cheiron you will see the ugly signs of modern tourist development and on the descent into the other village more nature and evidence of long abandoned mountain farming (see the photo with the sheep pen).

The path begins at signpost 13 east of the church on the very top of the hill of **Coursegoules**. It descends at first to a stream and then goes diagonally over terraced slopes in a northwesterly direction to **Chapelle St-Michel** (12th century). 400m after the chapel, at signpost 147, the steady climb begins round 22 hairpin bends to the western **Col de Coursegoules** (about 1410m); signpost 146. Now go along the almost 4km long east ridge to **Jérusalem** (1768m), the eastern summit of the Montagne du Cheiron. Cross over two distinct elevations on the east ridge, P. 1536m and La Croix de Verse (1706m). As the track is unclear and has infrequent waymarkings and cairns it is best to stay on the ridge or just to the right of it.

From Jérusalem on the north side go round the next elevation of the summit ridge to the **Sommet des Crêtes** (1766m) which is developed as well. You can either walk over or round it. Descend again on tracks into a hollow and up to the developed **Cime de Cheiron** (1778m), the highest summit of the Montagne du Cheiron (panorama guide).

At this point do not go down the slope, go over the west ridge which runs at first a little to the south. Go over various hilltops, often just to the right of the ridge, into a hollow with the remains of huts. Continue northwestwards round P. 1564m and descend through the little valley to the north of the ridge on a visibly better path down to the *GR 4* and signpost 194 in the **Col de Gréolières**. If in doubt, for example, in poor visibility, descend westwards through hollows from the Cime de Cheiron, until you come across the GR4. The path descends from the pass on numerous zigzags, finally goes left at the ruins of Hautes Gréolières and past the Chapelle Ste-Pétronille into the village of **Gréolières**.

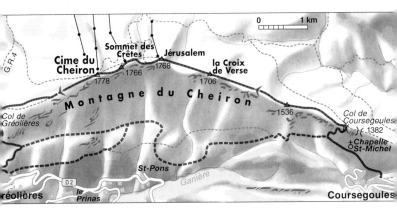

14 Circuit de Cipières

No view of the sea, instead a sea of stones in a green landscape

Cipières – Le Plan – Borie of Les Graus de Pons – Cipières

Starting point and destination: Cipières (744m) on the D 603 south of Gréolières and Montagne de Cheiron. Bus (rare!) from Grasse [TAM 512].
Walking time: 3 hours.
Ascent: 250m.
Distance: 10km.
Grade: No special requirements; yellow waymarkings.
Best time of year: (Too) hot in high summer, possible snow in winter.
Refreshments: In Cipières.
Accommodation: Château de Cipières; luxury hotel in the castle overlooking the village dating from the 13–18th century, tel: 04 93 59 98 00, fax: 04 93 59 98 02. In Gréolières; compare Walk 13.
Alternative: From the signpost 162 ascend southwards to a col and westwards with no paths to the Colle de Rougiès summit (1334m), falling away steeply to the south. Continue westwards to the Observatoire du C.E.R.G.A. (Centre d'études et de recherches géodynamiques et astronomique) which is at the edge of the Plateau de Calern; it's possible to visit the research centre founded in 1974; open daily in July and August to 14.30, otherwise on enquiry, tel: 04 93 41 23 04. The GR 4 goes over the karstic plateau of Calern back to Cipières; 5 hours, 16km, 600m in total.
Places of Interest: Agriculture, low-tech and away from the sea.
Map: TOP 25: Vallée de l'Estéron (3642 ET).
Tip: The emerald lizards on the edge of the path are not poisonous.
Adjoining walk: On the GR 4 from Cipières in 1 hour to Gréolières and up to the Montagne du Cheiron; compare Walk 13.

A short walk in a very impressive agricultural landscape at the edge of the karstic plateau of Calern, with a view of the 1000 metre high south face of the Montagne du Cheiron. The first half of the round walk deserves one star, but

Archaic construction: the stone igloo near Cipières reminds you of a forgotten era.

the return from the borie, the round stone construction, into the compact village of Cipières is simply sensational – just in its simplicity. The rough, stony terrain had little to offer in terms of agriculture so the farmers collected the stones and piled them up to make room for fields. Thousands upon thousands of stones were removed by hand and deposited in the right place – these artificial stone hills are called clapier. Tourists in the Côte d'Azur today walk straight through on the old path and are amazed that a landscape could have been shaped by its elements in such perfect harmony.

From the village square of **Cipières** go south onto the D 603. Go along this, past the Chapelle Saint-Claude for 1.5km as far as the hairpin bend (P. 729m) where you will see signpost 164. A little tarmac road leads southwards up to **Le Plan**. Go right at the fork in the road. The broad path winds over the small plateau (962m) and then for a long while keeps straight ahead. Where the path keeps to the left again, carry straight onto the signpost 161 of **Les Graus de Pons**. Now descend through the little wood, in the end keeping left towards the borie.

Go back up to the signpost and northwards through the stony agricultural landscape towards **Cipières**, where just before the village you come to the *GR 4*. At this point, at the edge of the village, turn right along a little tarmac road straight into the centre of the village with its narrow streets.

15 Gourdon

Along delightful paths into the tourist stronghold of the Loup gorge

Le Bar-sur-Loup – Chemin du Paradis – Gourdon – Le Bar-sur-Loup

Location: Grasse (338m); train and busses from Cannes Gare SNCF [TAM 600, 605, 610].
Starting point and destination: Le Bar-sur-Loup (289m) on the D2210 from Grasse to Vence. Bus from Grasse [TAM 510]. A bus goes from Grasse to Gourdon [TAM 512].
Walking times: Ascent 1¾ hours, descent 2¼ hours. Total time 4 hours.
Ascent: 420m.
Distance: 9km.
Grade: For those, for whom a stroll through the boutiques with perfume, handcrafts,

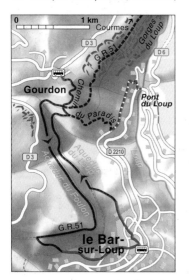

jewellry, wine and honey is not tiring enough. Remember to take a torch for the refreshing walk through the aqueduct tunnel. Waymarkings.
Best time of year: The *Chemin du Paradis* at midday in summer is like a path through purgatory.
Refreshments: Le Nid d'Aigle in Gourdon: the seats on top of the towers are some of the best on offer in the Côte d'Azur.
Accommodation: In Le Bar-sur-Loup: Hôtel Thébaïde, tel: 04 93 42 41 19; Camping Les Gorges du Loup with terraced slopes under olive trees, swimming pool. The 'patrone' helpfully displays many leaflets about walking in the area , tel/fax: 04 93 42 45 06.
Alternative: Go northwards on the *GR 51* along the Aqueduc du Foulon through the actual Gorges du Loup, best as far as Courmes (compare Walks 12, 45); 3 hours.
Places of Interest: The spring at the Aqueduc du Foulon and the one in Gourdon near the washing place, cool, shady and hardly used.
Map: TOP 25: Cannes – Grasse (3643 ET).
Tip: Gourdon château with historical museum, museum of naïve art and a park of the Versailles landscape designer Le Nôtre, open June – September 11-13.00 and 14-19.00, otherwise 14-18.00; closed on Tues. Big summer solstice festival, la Fête de St-Jean, in Le Bar-sur-Loup.
And: the Gorges du Loup is also a climbers' paradise; other information in *Escalade sur les Rives du Loup* by Gilbert Burzicchi and Pascal Maingon.
Adjoining walks: 16, 45.

On foot into one of the most famous villages perchés, those seemingly inaccessible villages on a hill. Gourdon, which guards the exit of the Loup gorge, is regularly besieged by tourists. The prospect of buying a souvenir in a place so full of character is as attractive as the panorama from this belvedere inland from the azure-blue coast. No wonder you meet the *GR of the Balcons de la Côte d'Azur* here as well. It runs along beside the Foulon aqueduct which was built in 1923 to water the Grasse flower fields where the essences were produced for the manufacture of perfume. You can smell the products in Gourdon and hear them being made as you go past one of the factories on the return to Le Bar-sur-Loup.

From the main road in **Le Bar-sur-Loup** (bus stop and car parks) go along Rue de la Salpetrière and through narrow alleyways, covered in places, up to the church and to the tourist office. Go right, past the Maison de Ville and gently ascend a little road, then left to the cemetary (red, white and blue arrows on the ground). You come to the Chapelle St-Claude. Immediately afterwards

Light and shade: view from Gourdon across Le Nid d'Aigle to the bends in the Chemin du Paradis.

leave the tarmac road to the left (signpost Gourdon) and ascend a stony path steeply up to the path along the Loup aqueduct (**Aqueduc du Loup**), which is not visible. Follow it as far as the crossroads with the **Chemin du Paradis** which comes up from the Pont du Loup. Go up to the *GR 51* and the **Aqueduc du Foulon**, the large and visible aqueduct (pipes). Here there's a spring with drinking water.

The Chemin du Paradis steadily winds up through steep terrain to **Gourdon** (760m). Go through the village to the viewing terrace. Descend the same way you came up to the **Foulon aqueduct**. Follow it along the valley, going through several tunnels. Above the Le Bar-sur-Loup the aqueduct goes round a rock projection. Just 1km later where the *GR 51* leaves the aqueduct on the right (Walk 16), you turn left onto a forest path. Continue along this, then on its tarmac continuation diagonally down to Chapelle St-Michel. Go along the Rue St-Michel to the gendarmerie in the village of **Le Bar-sur-Loup**. Descend through the old part of the village to the main road.

16 Haut Montet, 1335m – Colle du Maçon, 1417m

A very varied walk both through the historical and the contemporary

Le Bar-sur-Loup – Vallon de la Combe – Plateau de la Malle – Col de la Femme Morte – Le Haut Montet – Col de la Femme Morte – Colle du Maçon – Col du Ferrier – St-Vallier-de-Thiey

Starting point: Le Bar-sur-Loup (289m); compare Walk 15.
Destination: St-Vallier-de-Thiey (713m); compare Walk 17.
Walking times: Le-Bar-sur-Loup – quarry D 3 3 1¼ hours, climb up to the Col de la Femme Morte 2¾ hours, detour onto Le Haut Montet 1½-2 hours, climb up to the Colle du Maçon ¾ hours, descent to St-Vallier 2 hours. Total time about 8½ hours.
Ascent: About 1200m, descent about 800m.
Distance: 24km.
Grade: Strong lungs and legs, sturdy ankles, good route finding ability, strong nerves (as you cross the quarry). In bad visibility difficult route finding on the long west ridge of Haut Montet. No paths in

places, only occasionally marked with paint and cairns.
Best time of year: Spring and autumn.
Refreshments and accommodation: In Le Bar-sur-Loup: compare Walk 15. In St-Vallier: compare Walk 17.
Alternative: From the quarry continue along the *GR 51* as far as a crossroad after a go-kart track and ascend northwestwards. Or from Grasse go along the *GR 4* onto the Plateau de la Malle.
Places of Interest: The distant horizon above the karstic high plains and the vault in the cool stone igloo on the Col de la Femme Morte.
Map: TOP 25: Cannes – Grasse (3643 ET), Haute Siagne (3543 ET).
Tip: Take enough fluids with you.
Adjoining walks: 15, 17.

A long walk over varied terrain: through the stony old part of Le Bar-sur-Loup, over the Foulon aqueduct, through the dusty quarry, in the dark oak wood of the Vallon de la Combe, along the approach road to the Château La Malle which is blocked-off, without paths at the broad edge of the extensive Plateau de Caussols, on the shepherds' path to the Colle du Maçon, through the gorse undergrowth on its southern flank, on the stabilised mule track and the stone bridge below the Col du Ferrier, and finally on the Route Napoléon. Vive l'aventure!

From **Le Bar-sur-Loup** along the route described in Walk 15 as far as the aqueduct and to the *GR 51*. Go up along the *GR 51* to the D 3 (625m). Cross over the road to the quarry and go into the works site. Gently ascend the broad slope to the left of a dry stream bed. The main slope crosses the stream bed and ascends even more steeply. Cross over this on the main slope and ascend more steeply. At the hairpin bend go straight on across the bank and find (hopefully) an indistinct path. It leads into the valley along the slope (stony under foot and dry stone walls). You come to a bridge with metal girders which you cross over in spite of the fact that some of the wooden boards have rotted away. Climb up through the oak wood of the

Vallon de la Combe. At the top you come to a broad path, the *Chemin du Pilon de la Malle*. Take this path through fields and woods (at times beautiful spruce woods) onto a little tarmac road which crosses over the **Plateau de la Malle**. The *GR 4* joins in from the left. Coninue along the tarmac road as far as the entrance to the Domaine de la Malle, but please do not go in! Continue along the little road which turns off right to houses and the *GR 4* becomes an overgrown footpath in places. It leads up into the **Col de la Femme Morte** or **Col du Clapier** (1257m). The big borie is to be found on the left.

Go eastwards past the remains of huts, on a yellow marked path and partly through a wood up to the hilltop P.1310m. Now, mostly on grassy, karstic and undulating terrain with solitary trees, go eastwards past dolines up to **Le Haut Montet**. Finally on a gravel path go to the summit where you will find a ball-shaped antenna construction. Return on the same path to the **Col de la Femme Morte**. Go along the east ridge on the yellow-marked path, along by the private grounds of the Malle castle, to the **Colle du Maçon**. You will pass ruins on your way up to the summit.

From the summit go over the northwest ridge to a level area (about 1370m). Descend over the fairly steep southwest flank (bushes and stones) with bands of rock on the left and a wood on the right. When you are lower than the rock bands descend southeastwards towards the square house with the flat roof, on tracks over terrain with bushes and the occasional tree. Before the house you come to a spring. Below the house you meet a field path which you descend to a smaller house at a crossroads. Go right, along a broad path and past a private borie, to the **Col du Ferier** (1039m). Just above the road turn left onto on old path which leads uphill on the left side of the valley. It crosses the road at the point where the road comes over to the same side. The path descends towards a new residential district and goes along the Chemin d'Entrevaux to reach the Route Napoléon. Walk along this to **St-Vallier-de-Thiey**. The pump room can be found where the road turns off to St-Cézaire-sur-Siagne.

17 The old Route Napoléon

Along the best maintained section of the imperial path

St-Vallier-de-Thiey – Le Vieux Pont/Siagne – Escragnolles

Starting point: St-Vallier-de-Thiey (713m), the first village after Grasse on the N 85, the Route Napoléon. Bus from Grasse [TAM 810 Grasse – St-Vallier].

Destination: Escragnolles (1039m) lies 17km northwest of St-Vallier. Bus from Grasse via St-Vallier to St-Auban [TAM 800; Mon. to Sat. morning and evening service, no buses running on Sun. and Bank Holidays]. Large car park with snack bar in Escragnolles La Colette; from there it's best to hitchhike back to St-Vallier on today's Route Napoléon.

Walking time: 3 hours.

Ascent: 500m, descent a good 150m.

Distance: 10km.

Grade: Easy walking.

Best time of year: Beginning of March.

Refreshments: The Grand Pré of St-Vallier is a popular spot for a picnic.

Accommodation: In St-Vallier-de-Thiey: Relais Impérial on the Route Napoléon, tel: 04 92 60 36 36; Camping Parc des Arbois, tel: 04 93 42 63 89.

Alternative: Via Grotte de Baume Obscure: follow the signs on roads to the limestone caves, open daily from Easter to 30th September, 10-18.00, tel: 04 93 42 61 63. On mostly concrete paths to the entrance (guided tours). Descend on yellow-marked paths to a dry stream bed, go along this on the right and sometimes on the left. Before the valley hollow begins to descend noticeably, go left onto a good, yellow-marked path which you follow to the *GR 510*. Go northwards along an aqueduct to the little road which goes down to the Pont Vieux.

Places of Interest: Historic paving stones.

Map: TOP 25: Haute Siagne (3543 ET).

Tip: The book *Vivre l'autentique Route Napoléon* by Camille Bartoli (Éditions TAC Motifs, 1994) shows exactly where Napoléon went. If you want a guided tour: *Randonnée historique sur les traces de Napoléon et ses hussards*; 1. a half-day from St-Vallier to Escragnolles, 2. a half-day from Escragnolles to Séranon; at Préalpes 06 in 06630 Gréolières, tel: 04 93 59 98 81.

Adjoining walks: 16; 18 (on the *GR 510* to St-Cézaire-sur-Siagne).

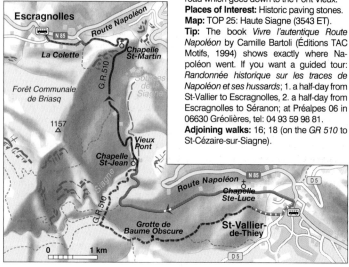

Traces of history: Napoléon marched up to the left on 2ⁿᵈ March.

The 31km long Route Napoléon from Golfe-Juan via Cannes, Grasse, Castellane, Digne, Sisteron and Gap to Grenoble is the most famous country road in France. On his return from his exile on Elba with his followers Napoléon landed in the Golfe-Juan near Cannes on the first of March, 1815. On the next day he began the march over the Alps. On the 7th March he arrived in Grenoble to cries of 'Long live the Emperor!' and his rule of 100 days began in Paris. Today's road is not totally identical to the route which Napoléon took. For example the old Route Napoléon between St-Vallier-de-Thiey and Escragnolles runs on the opposite side of the gorge-like valley through which the Siagne flows. And just at the most dangerous point the historic path has been preserved with its dry stone walls, edging and paving stones. Foreward, march!

The little tarmac road which runs westwards, below the Chapelle Ste-Luce starts on the hill of the big meadow in **St-Vallier-de-Thiey**, 100m north of the point where the road turns off to St-Cézaire. It goes up and down along the edge of the Siagne gorge and then down into the gorge itself. The *GR 510* joins from the left. Stay left at the fork in the road and you come to the Chapelle St-Jean and after that to the **Vieux Pont** (589m). Walk along the access road to the Léchen farm where you finally meet the imperial path in its original form. It is best preserved below and above the derelict Chapelle St-Martin. Soon afterwards you reach **Escragnolles**. If you want to go to the big car park on the new Route Napoléon, climb straight up to it, but to get to the bus stop you need to stay on the path below the road and then ascend a small tarmac road into the village.

18 Gorges de la Siagne

Swimming, not in the sea, but in the river below a medieval bridge

Pont de la Siagne – Chapelle St-Saturnin – Pont des Tuves in the Siagne gorge – St-Cézaire-sur-Siagne

Location: Grasse (338m). Busses from Cannes and Nice.

Starting point: Pont de la Siagne (110m) on the D 2562 from Grasse to Draguignan. Bus from Grasse Gare Routière via Peymeinade [Line 2P from STGA, tel: 04 93 64 88 84].

Destination: St-Cézaire-sur Siagne (477m) on the eastern edge of the Siagne gorge; D 13 from Grasse, D 5 from St-Vallier-de-Thiey. Bus from Grasse via Gabris and Spéracède to St-Cézaire [Transports Autocars Côte d'Azur – Vallée du Loup; no service on Sundays and Bank Holidays; TAM 520 Grasse – St-Cézaire].

Walking times: Pont de la Siagne – Pont des Tuves 2 hours, ascent to St-Cézaire 1 hour. Total time 3 hours.

Ascent: Just under 500m, descent about 100m.

Distance: 6km.

Grade: Too stony and steep for pure beach walkers, marked yellow and sometimes red and white.

Best time of year: All year round, but best in the summer for swimming.

Refreshments: In Pont de la Siagne.

Accommodation: In St-Cézaire: Hôtel Les Chênes Blancs, tel: 04 93 60 20 09; La Petite Auberge, tel/fax: 04 93 60 26 60. Camping El Perdido, tel: 04 93 60 20 76.

Alternatives: Start in St-Cézaire-sur-Siagne: either there and back to the tufa bridge or do the following nicer round walks: 1) From the Pont des Tuves along a yellow-marked path on the west side of the river as far as a stone bridge and returning on terraced slopes, crossing over the Canal de la Siagne again into the village; 3 hours. 2) From St-Cézaire on one of the other marked paths in the direction of Pont de la Siagne or just to the Chapelle St-Saturnin.

Places of Interest: Old paths, olive groves on sheer slopes in southern heat.

Map: TOP 25: Haute Siagne (3543 ET).

Tip: At the end of the feasible path from the Pont des Tuves along the right hand bank down the river to Pont de la Siagne you meet a private road unfortunately (it's your own responsibility).

Adjoining walk: 17.

You may not believe your senses, but everything you see and smell as you are walking, you have to believe is real. And then you dive into the green river below the elegant and unexpected tufa bridge. A combination of wild nature and human culture which can also be found on this path into the village which clings to the edge of the gorge.

The marked path begins immediately opposite the bus stop in **Pont de la Siagne**, just above the bridge and the restaurant. There's a signpost with the three different routes to St-Cézaire. Ascend along a small road, a path and then again a small road up past houses into the gorge. After the bridge over a stream keep to the right, go up a few zigzags and at the next fork keep right

Freshwater: the Siagne separates the coastal départements of Alpes-Maritimes and Var.

again. Immediately afterwards two paths turn off right to St-Cézaire, one via La Valmoura, the other via Bergeris. You stay on the third one, the red and white marked path (*GR 510*), descend a short way and then walk on the level to the beautiful pump room. Continue on the level in the wood past some ruins, to a fork. Descend left to the **Chapelle St-Saturnin**. Return to the fork and go along the path into the gorge to a water channel (about 240m) which provides the supply of water to Grasse and Cannes. The marked path crosses the channel and ascends diagonally, going over a partly broken wooden bridge and then to a fork (P. 281m). The signpost points left to the Pont des Tuves. This is the way you return to the water channel. It looks possible to follow the channel, thereby avoiding the sweat-making diversion. Now go down to the Siagne and up the river to the **Pont des Tuves** (165m). Return to the signpost at P. 281m and along the path over the terraces with the olive trees up to **St-Cézaire-sur-Siagne**. You reach the village between the cemetery and the church. The viewing point at the edge of the gorge is just to the north of the village.

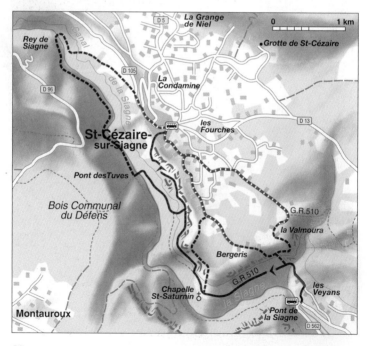

In the land of the sun: the Canal de la Siagne takes water to Grasse and Cannes.

Estérel – red cliffs

'The long red coast falls into the blue sea which appears violet. It is strange, rugged and pretty, with countless peaks and bays, with individual and alluring rocks evoking a world of fantasy. On the flanks of these amazing mountains there are pine forests reaching up to the granite tops which look like castles, towns and stone armies, all pursuing one another. And the sea at its feet is so clear that, in some places, you can see down to the sandy sea bed and the plants.' This is how Guy de Maupassant describes the Estérel coast between Cannes and St-Raphaël in his refreshing 1888 travelogue *Sur l'eau* about a sailing trip on the Côte d'Azur on his yacht Bel-Ami. But for you it's the other way around: you view the blue waves from the red cliffs instead of the Massif d'Estérel from the sea.

The Corniche de l'Estérel: the kind of Côte d'Azur you will not often see between Nice and Toulon. Only the railway and a road built in 1903 wind their way along the coastline of the Estérel mountains and jostle for position below the sheer summit looming high above the surf. This is a walkers' paradise with many (marked and unmarked) paths. One breathtaking walk goes over the seven outer peaks of the Massif de l'Estérel (Walk 20). Cars race against trains whose recurrance punctuates the day's progress over the last summits on this part of the alpine arc. Only a few minutes by train from the film metropolis of Cannes you can walk from station to station, from mountain to mountain. At the end you come to the Anthéor viaduct which is almost the same colour as the Estérel castellations. The yellow beach with the blue sea is in front of the viaduct and behind it is a restaurant where you can drink 'sirop de menthe', ice-cold and green. As you enjoy this drink the blue and white TGV crosses the red arched bridge: a beautiful sight!

The highest summit of the Estérel mountains, the Mont Vinaigre, rises only 614 metres above the Mediterranean. Its low height in actual metres and its nearness to the beach encourage false opinion that it isn't part of the Alps. It is, without doubt, as much a part of the Alps as the Viennese forest at the other end. Alpine reference books merely disagree as to whether it is part of the Maritime Alps or the Provence Alps. One thing for certain is that the Estérel forms one of the oldest sections in the alpine arc. It is, according to the *Companion Guide to the South of France* by Archibald Lyall, 1963, part of the remains 'of the so-called Tyrrhenian plate, of a continent which rose up about 600 million years ago in the place of today's Mediterranean – just as old as the Massif Central and the Central Iberian Plateau. Some 'peaks' of this sunken continent can still be seen in the sea, such as the islands of Corsica, Sardinia and the Balearics.' You can see Corsica from the highest Estérel cliffs on a clear day and often on the horizon beyond the white shores of Cannes, the 3000ers of the Maritime Alps covered in snow in winter and spring. There are some wonderful level walks on its off-shore islands, the Îles

de Lérins (Walk 19), and they can be done at any time of year.

The most well-known summit of the Massif d'Estérel is the Pic du Cap Roux, a peak covered in bushes, surrounded by steep, sharp-edged porphyry cliffs of volcanic origin which give it a distinctive appearance. It has earned the honour, and also the panorama guide at the very top, put up by the Touring Club of France (not the Alpine Club). The green Michelin guide *Côte d'Azur* gives the view of Pic du Cap Roux three stars, so it's 'worth a journey'.

The Estérel Massif and the coastline are ideal for cycling and a mountain bike is an advantage. You can, for example, do the route by bike from Théoule-sur-Mer to Anthéor as well as to Agay, going round the summits instead, with the exception of the Pic de l'Ours. The highest summit of the Estérel is as accessible as some of the deep gorges. During the day the coast road is fairly busy and also the road northwards from Agay is a popular link road. The rest of the road and path network, however, offers pure enjoyment for the cyclist. The enjoyable drive round the Pic d'Aurelle at sunrise and a quick walk up to its viewing point in order to hang over the ledge. It is as unforgettable as the drive along the tarmac road, closed to traffic, from the Pointe du Cap Roux towards the Rocher de Saint-Barthélemy. Be careful as you balance high up on its exposed path (Walk 21). In short: bike and hike en toute perfection. Or to put it a different way: vive les vacances sportives!

La vie en rose: view down from Rocher de St-Barthélemy to the coast road and the railway with the TGV just crossing over.

19 Îles de Lérins

Two quiet, secluded walks on sacred islands just off-shore from Cannes

Île Sainte-Marguerite and Île Saint-Honorat

Child's play: old steps in Fort Royal on the Île Sainte-Marguerite – one of the few noticeable ascents.

Starting point and destination: Cannes (0m), Gare Maritime at the little harbour opposite the Palais des Festivales. Many crossings; it's best to book the daily crossing to both islands in advance. The crossing to Ste-Marguerite and the continuation to St-Honorat take 15 minutes each.

Information: Tel: 04 93 38 66 33.

Walking times: Ste-Marguerite 2¾ hours, St-Honorat 1 hour.

Ascent: Slight.

Distance: Ste-Marguerite 8½km, St-Honorat 3½km.

Grade: No special requirements.

Best time of year: All year round.

Refreshments: Restaurants on both islands; pretty picnic spots.

Accommodation: Numerous hotels in Cannes.

Places of Interest: The five storey, fortified monastery on St-Honorat, which stands almost in the water, is perhaps the finest building which has ever been built on the azure-blue coast, more harmonious and powerful, unique and isolated as any villa between Menton and Marseille.

Map: TOP 25: Cannes – Grasse (3643 ET).

Tip: Small bays for swimming, but please not in the nude. Fort Royal with the Musée de la Mer (closed midday). Monastère Fortifié open daily 9-12 and 14-16.45.

From the mooring on Ste-Marguerite you first follow the nature trail to the fortress. The most famous cell on the Côte d'Azur is to be found here. This is where the man in the iron mask was kept prisoner in the 17th century and whose identity is still a mystery today. You can enjoy the view from the fortress walls of Cannes where, since May 1946, stars are photographed at the most important film festival of the world.

After walking round the island of Ste-Marguerite you take the boat to the island of St-Honorat further out to sea. The sacred dignitaries founded the first monastery in 410 and the island is still inhabited and run by monks today. Walk round this island and you come to the Monastère Fortifié, the medieval fortification of the monks. From the battlements you can look across to the silhouette of the Estérel Massif, which looks like a wedge, serrated at the top, pushing into the azure-blue surface.

Ste-Marguerite: Go round the island in a clockwise direction. You can walk from the mooring right beside the shore to the Fort Royal, but it's nicer to start on the *Sentier botanique*, just above the mooring, as it curves round to the south and brings you back to the fortress. You can familiarise yourself with the vegetation on the island (and the Côte d'Azur) on the nature trail. It's not especially well marked and if you get lost, go eastwards in the wood up to the Allée des Eucalyptus and then north to reach the fortress. Where the nature trail meets the fortress walls either go left to get a good view of the fort (and then return to the fork later) or go immediately to the right of it down to the sea. Now begin the walk round the coastal path. It goes to the Pointe de la Convention where there's a bunker. Go along the south coast to the Pointe du Dragon, then continue between the coast and the Batéguier pond to the Pointe de Batéguier (you can also reach the north coast by staying on the western bank of the pond). Return quickly to the mooring.

St-Honorat: From the mooring walk round the eastern part of the island in a clockwise direction to the Monastère Fortifié and to the monastery. It's now best to return to the mooring through the lavender fields and round the western part of the island back to the monastery.

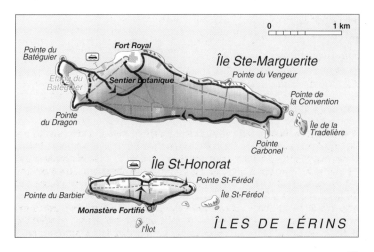

20 Les Balcons de l'Estérel

Summits on parade where the mountains meet the sea

Théoule-sur-Mer – Sommet des Grosses Grues – Sommet des Petites Grues – Pic de l'Ours – Dent de l'Ours – Pic d'Aurelle – Pic du Cap Roux – Le St-Pilon – Anthéor Plage

Starting point: Théoule-sur-Mer (0m) on the rail and bus route St-Raphaël – Cannes; the bus stop is in the centre and the station is to the south. Compare Walk 22.

Destination: Anthéor Plage (0m); bus stop below the viaduct, station to the south; compare Walk 22.

Walking times: Ascent to the Sommet des Grosses Grues 2 hours, over the Sommet des Petites Grues onto the Pic de l'Ours 1¼ hours, over the Dent de l'Ours onto the Pic d'Aurelle 1½ hours, on to the Pic du Cap Roux 1¾ hours, traverse to the St-Pilon ¾ hours, descent to Anthéor 1 hour. Total time a good 8 hours or more…

Ascent: About 1200m.

Distance: 21km.

Grade: Difficult walk (tricky ground, route-finding) over seven summits on the coastal flank of the Massif de l'Estérel. If you leave out the Dent de l'Ours and especially the Saint-Pilon (both where you need to do some easy climbing), the ridge walk is significantly easier (paths usually marked, but in a variety of ways) and also shorter.

Best time of year: Too hot in high summer.

Refreshments: No water to drink on the way, so take enough fluids with you.

Accommodation: Compare Walks 21 and 22. The Auberge de Jeunesse of Trayas is below the Col Notre-Dame, tel: 04 93 75 40 23.

Alternative: From almost all the dips in the ridge there are paths leading down to the coast with bus stops and Le Trayas station.

Places of Interest: Walking above the most beautiful section of railway on the coast.

Map: TOP 25: Fréjus – St-Raphaël (3544 ET)

Tip: Neither camping, lighting a fire nor smoking is allowed on the Estérel massif.

Adjoining walks: 21, 45.

A heart's beat away from the hiking paths is the beach, where new arrivals realise that the Côte d'Azur really does live up to its reputation as a holiday destination without clothes. The Saint-Pilon, with its bright red, vertical flanks, seems to deter any approach in walking shoes.

The ascent to the first summit begins by walking along the noisy road (do not follow the *GR 51*) from the railway station into the centre of **Théoule-sur-Mer**. Now go inland on the red and white GR 51 into the Vallon de l'Autel and up to the **Col de Théoule**. Continue along the dusty fire-protected road to the **Col du Trayas**, taking shortcuts across its wide bends on unmarked paths. On its north side join a small road again to the **Col de la Cadière** and go on a path over the western ridge to the **Sommet des Grosses Grues** (441m) with its antenna.

Continue through undergrowth for a short way seawards to get a view of the sea. Follow the state-owned path and the green and white marked national forest boundary over the **Sommet des Petites Grues** (411m) to the **Col Notre-Dame**, where you leave the *GR 51*. Go on a stony path over the north

Resisting: St-Pilon from the Col de St-Pilon – the gully is the way up and down.

ridge to the **Pic de l'Ours** (492m), the highest summit above the Estérel coast which is occupied by a television tower. In spite of this you can reach the highest point by climbing up left onto a rock at the end of the approach road about 50m before the tower and sneaking up to the barbed wire fence. Go under the fence on the north side to the north ridge and down the other side into the **Brèche de la Dent de l'Ours** (it doesn't have a name on the map). From the crossroads go along the path to the approximately 30m high red **Dent de l'Ours** (416m).

Go past it on the left until a track goes up right to a ramp on the northwest face. Climb up this ramp to a rock spike, keeping left over a rock step, to reach the highest point of the 'bear's tooth' (grade I, a few metres of grade II). On the west and south flanks of Pic de l'Ours you come to the **Col des Lentisques**, from where you can make a detour to the **Pic d'Aurelle** (322m), the lowest of the seven summits and for this reason the one which brings you closest to the sea.

Return back down the ascent path down for a short way, but then take the path to **Baisse des Sangliers** where you find a path above the road. You come finally to the **Col de l'Évêque** (159m) where three roads and three paths cross each other. Go along the path on the north ridge to the Col de Cardinal and go across the north flank up to the **Pic du Cap Roux** (453m), which you eventually reach from the south (panorama guide). Descend to the **Col du Cap Roux**.

Two paths separate here to go onto the St-Pilon. The easier route goes round

St-Jean-de-Cannes

la Napoule

Théoule-sur-Mer

Pointe de l'Aiguille

Maure Vieille

439
Sommet Pelet

Ravin des Trois Termes

Col du Trayas

241   245   123

Col de la Cadière

441   Sommet des Grosses Grues

Col de Théoule

N 98

la Galère

411   Sommet des Petites Grues

G.R.51

le Trayas Supérieur

G.R.51

Dent de l'Ours
416

324
Col Notre-Dame

Miramar

Pointe de l'Esquillon

Lac de l'Écureuil

492   Pic de l'Ours

Col des Lentisques   261

Baisse des Sangliers

322
Pic d'Aurelle

le Trayas

Col de l'Évêque

159

Pic du Cap Roux

Pointe de Maubois

359
le St-Pilon   453

Col du Cap Roux

Pointe du Cap Roux

Col du St-Pilon   445
283   Rocher de St-Barthélemy

Pointe de l'Observatoire

203

Plateau d'Anthéor

N 98

Viaduc   Anthéor Plage

Anthéor

Île des Vieilles

Corniche de l'Esterel

0   1 km

Picturesque: sunset on the Col de l'Evêque – and above the Îles de Lérins.

this very striking and highest rock of the Massif de l'Estérel along a path on the south side to the Col du St-Pilon, from where you can go up the descent path.

The other path is as follows: from Cap Roux go on a track to the rock tooth Quiquillon (not named on the map) and round its north side. This leads up to the ridge again where it becomes an imaginary path: a few non-vegetated patches one after the other result in a sort of path which crosses over the nearest rock towers on the shady side and reaches the ridge again. Now it runs through the undergrowth just below the eastern summit of Saint-Pilon, but is suddenly overgrown with prickly bushes and there is no way through. A band of rock saves you from turning back and you climb over this onto a scree slope. It's a laborious climb and at the top it narrows into a gully which you scramble through into a gap and over a short rock step up to the highest point of **Saint-Pilon** (445m).

Return to the scree and stumble downwards, keeping to the left on very loose tracks. Where the stones give way to vegetation it widens out into a path which forks soon afterwards. Take the right hand turn-off to the **Col du St-Pilon**. Go along the main path to the **Plateau d'Anthéor** and to a picnic spot. On the southern edge of the small plateau you will find (hopefully) the path which is marked on the map but unmarked on the ground and descends southeastwards through a little valley, at first flanked on both sides by rocks, to the railway lines and the coast road. Continue on this across the bay of **Anthéor**, until the access road to the station branches off to the right.

21 Pic du Cap Roux, 453m

At the furthest reach of the Alps: religious and tourist places of pilgrimage

Coast road – (Rocher de St-Barthélemy –) Col du St-Pilon – La Sainte-Baume with grotto chapel – Pic du Cap Roux – coast road

Location: Anthéor-Plage on the Corniche de l'Estérel; compare Walk 22.

Starting point and Destination: Cap Roux bus stop (37m) on the RN 98 between Anthéor and Le Trayas, at the Pointe de l'Observatoire and near a level-crossing; compare Walk 22.

Walking times: Ascent and descent over the Col de St-Pilon to Sainte Baume 1¼ hours, visiting the chapel in a cave ½ hour, ascent onto the Pic du Cap Roux 1 hour, descent to the coast 1 hour. Total time 3 ¾ hours.

Ascent: 550m.

Distance: 10km.

Grade: Being sure-footed is an advantage for the Circuit du Pic du Cap Roux. Way-markings of different colours.

Best time of year: All year round; best in spring and early summer.

Refreshments: Sainte-Baume-Quelle with marvellously fresh water.

Accommodation: Hotels and holiday flats in Agay, Anthéor, Le Trayas, Miramar and Théoule-sur-Mer. Recommended is the 'Le Viaduc' campsite in Anthéor Plage, open from Easter to end of September, tel: 04 94 44 82 31. Other campsites in Agay and Le Dramont; compare Walk 22.

Alternative: Rocher de St-Barthélemy (203m): from the col (157m) go over and along rocks to the summit which is covered in iron stumps (grade I-II, very exposed);

finally over a few boulders to the highest point. If you prefer to get there by train you have 2 starting points: from Anthéor on the route described in Walk 20 to the Plateau Anthéor and then to the Rocher de St-Barthélemy or straight onto the Col du St-Pilon; or start in Le Trayas from where a gravel path leads up to the Col de l'Évêque. You can also walk from one station to another.

Places of Interest: Sharp-edged porphyry, knotty cork oaks, aromatic pines and a long way below train, road and bays for swimming (especially beautiful near the Pointe de l'Observatoire).

Map: TOP 25: Fréjus – St-Raphaël (3544 ET).

Tip: Neither camping, lighting a fire or smoking is allowed in the Estérel massif.

Adjoining walk: 20.

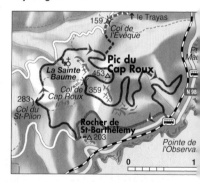

The rock of St-Barthélemy is a red monolith almost perpendicular above the coastal cliffs which up to the middle of the nineties was traversed by a short climb. Mountaineers will not want to lose this delightful path. Pilgrims visit a chapel in a cave hidden on the side that is away from the sea where Saint-Honorat lived before the foundation of the monastery on the smaller island of Lérins near Cannes.

From **Cap Roux bus stop** go up onto the tarmac forest road which is closed to cars. Large areas of pine forests burnt down in the summer of 2000. After a bend the road leads westwards across the slopes of the Pic du Cap Roux and climbs up to a col (157m) west of the Rocher de St-Barthélemy. Ascend a path up to the **Col du St-Pilon** (283m).

On the north side a path descends to **La Sainte-Baume** (170m), the place of pilgrimage a few metres above a road. A path nearby begins to ascend to the north and you soon reach the turn-off to the chapel in a cave. A beautifully constructed path leads upwards to a rock tower (Le Pilon). Traverse below this (one slightly exposed point) to a tower with a gateway. Go through and down some steps to the **Chapelle de la Grotte Saint-Honorat** (240m).

Return to the turn-off (190m) and ascend the north flank to the **Pic du Cap Roux** (panorama guide). Descend to the Col du Cap Roux, then go south (the first few metres are not easily visible), and later on descend eastwards to a fork in the path above a railway tunnel. From here quickly return to the Calanque du Maubois bus stop or on an undercut path back to the starting point.

Inviting: gateway at Ste-Baume chapel in the cave – Pic de l'Ours on the left.

22 Cap du Dramont

A typical place on the Estérel coast with beautiful views and bays

Le Dramont – Pointe du Dramont – Sémaphore – Belvédère de la Batterie – Camp Long

Starting point and destination: Le Dramont train station on the St-Raphaël – Cannes line. Thanks to the local train there is no need for a car for the walks on the Corniche de l'Estérel. It is recommended that you write down the local time-table at each bus stop. There's a regular bus service 'Ligne de la Corniche d'Or' along the coast road, Route Nationale 98, from St-Raphaël to Cannes; information in St-Raphaël: tel: 04 94 95 16 71 or 04 94 53 78 46.
Walking time: Just under 2 hours.
Ascent: Just under 200m.
Distance: 5km.
Grade: Easy; a few sections demand some sure-footedness; waymarkings in several places.
Best time of year: All year round.
Refreshments: Beautiful restaurant on the Plage de Camp Long.
Accommodation: On Cap du Dramont there are 2 campsites: Les Campéoles, tel: 04 94 82 07 68; Royal, tel: 04 94 82 00 20. In Agay the Les Rives de l'Agay campsite open from the end of Feb., tel: 04 94 82 02 74. In Fréjus thr Auberge de Jeunesse, tel: 04 94 52 18 75.
Alternative: Begin the walk from Camp

Long bus stop – or finish it there; use the entrance to the Plage de Camp Long.
Places of Interest: Amaranth-red and azure-blue.
Map: TOP 25: Fréjus – St-Raphaël (3544 ET).
Tip: Cap du Dramont ist also a climbing area with numerous short routes between 5 and 7b+ in four areas; more information in the topo guide *Escalade dans les Maures et l'Estérel* by Christian Rive.

Belvédère de la Batterie is the name of one of the viewing points of Cap du Dramont: panorama lovers and the military have both found a home on this stretch of the Estérel coast. The 36th US infantry regiment landed on Dramont beach on the 15th August, 1944 and the walk goes past the memorial. The square tower on the small Île d'Or remains in view for a long time. Was it a fortress or a gaol where members of Gaspard de Bresse's band of robbers were kept prisoners? These 18th century bandits had a firm grip on Estérel as well as the thoughts and money of those who travelled there. After that the prisoners who had escaped from Toulon, and later the French resistance movement, made the mountains with the forests and ravines into a hideaway.

Secret place: for those acquainted with Tintin, the island of gold is the 'Île Noire'.

From **Le Dramont** station go along the coast road towards Agay until the access road to the anchorage point, Abri du Poussaï, branches off right after the campsite 'Les Campéoles'.

Continue along this for 300m then turn up left onto the marked hikers' path which leads round Cap du Dramont in an anti-clockwise direction sometimes high above the red cliffs. Opposite the Île d'Or some cul-de-sacs go down to bays. On the seaward side, above the deeply eroded Mare Règue, turn left onto the path which leads to the col (88m) between both of the 'summits' of Cap du Dramont. First of all go along on asphalt access road to the **lighthouse** which is fenced off (136m). You come to a viewing platform on the west side along a partly stabilised path. Then return to the col and the **Bélvédère de la Batterie** (107m), a former fortress and today the site for an ugly installation.

Go back down to the col and continue the round walk. You come to a car park just to the south above the **Plage de Camp Long**. Now either go to the beach or to the bus stop on the road west of the beach approach road or return along the path inland of Cap du Dramont, meeting your original path again at the Maison forestière.

Massif des Maures: green waves

'The little towns of Sollies, Cures and Pignans, which you reach one after the other, distinguish themselves with nothing other than the dirt in the alleyways which are filled with manure.' Tourist operators would not be happy to read such a description – but when the Karlsruhe priest Christian Friedrich Mylius hiked from Hyères through the three small towns to Fréjus with his note book, tourism was in no need of any beautifying organisations. And German speakers who wanted to travel to the Côte d'Azur – this expression did not exist then either – were pointed in the direction of tourist writers like Mylius who had left his home town on June 28, 1818. His *Picturesque journey on foot through the South of France and a part of northern Italy* appeared in four volumes in the years 1818/1819. The author did not like the valley where Pignans lies: 'Nothing here is more monotonous than the view of the land-scape. You are continually walking in forests of olive trees covering the broad valley and the hillsides.'

Little has changed about this assessment today: The valley between Hyères and Fréjus lies away from the streams of tourists, but not away from the busy communications network. The railway line from Marseille to Nice and Genua was made to go inland for the only time on the French-Italian Riviera, exactly like the motorway later. The reason for this was the Massif des Maures.

This densely wooded low mountain region, a maximum of 20km wide, stretches for over 55km. The northern chain is the longest of the three parallel main chains and also has the highest summit, La Sauvette (779m). The southern chain is the most well-known because it contains places like Le Lavandou and Cavalaire-sur-Mer on its seaward side. This section of the Côte d'Azur is also called the Corniche de Maures. The northeastern part of the Massif de Maures is called Les Petites Maures, while the very small Maurettes lie on the southwestern tip, right at the edge of Hyères. The Massif des Maures is ancient like the Estérel mountains, therefore also no longer of great height. Erosion has worn away the crystalline rock.

The name comes from the Provençal 'maouro' which means dark tree. In a footnote Mylius gives another explanation for the name: 'Moorish mountains (Montagnes des Maures) got their name from the Saracens who settled here in the 9th and 10th centuries after they had landed in the Gulf of Grimaud and established themselves in the mountain castle of Fraxinet opposite the small town of St. Tropes.' In the year 973 the Saracens were driven out of Fraxinet, today's La Garde-Freinet. If you want to admire the view of the gulf of St-Tropez from the castle, follow Walk 24.

Not all the paths in the Massif des Maures harmonise so perfectly with nature as does this secret path. Because the woods, once so impenetrable, kept burning down, kilometre long firebreak roads were constructed. The most beautiful of these important link roads is the one on the southern-most green

Laisser-faire: view from the mountain chain nearest to the sea of the receding hills of the Maures massif; in the summer a symphony of green, in the autumn a play of colours like in the procession of flowers.

wave. From here you can enjoy a wonderful view of the blue waves, although the whole stretch is tarmac and is consequently only an advantage for cycling. Those on foot should visit instead the pilgrims' trail to the Notre-Dame de Constance (Walk 26) in Bormes-les-Mimosas above Le Lavandou, best when the mimosa promisea golden yellow spring. The robust plant originating in Australia flowers from January to March. Every year ten thousand tons of little gold balls are harvested and eight million bunches are sent to all parts of the world. The perfume industry of Grasse processes the rest.

The characteristic nature of the Massif des Maures is its expanse and tranquility. In order to experience this to the full walkers should become familiar with the *GR 90* between Le Lavandou and Notre-Dames des Anges (767m) above Pignans. They will then come to Collobrières, the capitale des Maures. This pretty, lively village lies between the north and central chain of the Massif des Maures, surrounded by extensive sweet chestnut and oak woods. The bark of the cork oak is made into souvenirs amongst other things, the edible sweet chestnuts are crystallised for marrons glacés, but can also be enjoyed as ice cream, jam, sweets, cream or liqueur. An ancient willow tree bows over the Maison de Marron just by the Pont Vieux, which dates from the 12th century.

Above Collobrières the Carthusian monastery of Verne (Walk 25) is hidden in the middle of extensive cork oak woods and sweet chestnut groves. It's a pity that Mylius didn't go there. A stop at the cloister-lined cemetery would have impressed him as much as the view out of the window: the deep blue gulf of Saint-Tropez with its white ships so near and yet so far.

23 Rocher de Roquebrune, 373m

Partly secured ladder reaching heavenwards on red castellations above the motorway

Roquebrune-sur-Argens – Rocher de Roquebrune – Col du Facteur – GR 51 – Roquebrune-sur-Argens

Starting point and destination: Roquebrune-sur-Argens (20m) on the bus route St-Raphaël – Fréjus – Le Muy – Draguignan [Forum Cars, Fréjus Infobus, tel: 04 94 53 78 46]. Also the Ligne Urbaine Roquebrune-sur-Argens – La Bouverie – Les Issambres – San-Peire-sur-Mer [SVA, tel: 04 94 45 51 21]. No easy access by train as there are few local trains and the station is not closeby.

Walking times: Ascent and descent 2 hours each.
Ascent: About 450m.
Distance: 10km.
Grade: The east-west traverse is very difficult. East ridge: short sections of climbing (grade I), the most difficult places protected with cables. The route is mostly well-marked in blue, but you still need good route-finding ability. Discreetly placed white stars indicate a direct line over the highest points of the ridge (climbing routes). The descent over the west ridge to the Col du Facteur is a bit easier. The normal ascent from the south is the easiest, but it's still graded black.

Best time of year: All year round; hot in summer. Not in damp conditions due to moss-covered rocks. Best very early in the morning when the towers of the east ridge light up and the plain is still lying in shadow.
Stops and accommodation: Villages Hôtel, tel: 04 94 45 45 00. Camping Le Moulin des Iscles is well-tended, tel: 04 94 45 70 74.

Alternative: Normal path: there are 2 places to turn off from the *GR 51* if you come from Roquebrune-sur-Argens. The first time is at  the cairn west of three similarly beautiful paths through a mimosa wood. The second time (marked yellow) at the fork east of P. 192m. Then the path ascends through the lightly vegetated south flank, goes across a reddish slab and then goes steeply up over stony ground to the summit ridge. A total of 3 hours for the climb up the normal path.

Places of Interest: The whole setting of the Notre Dame de Roquette (pilgrims' chapel from the 16th century) at the northern foot of the western ridge of the Rocher de Roquebrune; the chapel of St-Jean is tucked away in an enormous rocky cleft, and only virtuous young women can get through the Saint-Trou (and slim walkers with a torch). The approach is easiest from the little road parallel to the motorway. You can also reach this mysterious place from the Col du Facteur on very overgrown and adventurous paths.

Map: TOP 25: Les Arcs – Le Muy (3544 OT).
Tip: The Fête de la Randonnée takes place in mid-June with different walks, also on the rocks round the village. Information from the Office du Tourisme, tel: 04 94 45 72 70, or at the Club d'Escalade et de Randonnée on Boulevard Jean Jaurès.

From above: view from the main summit of the secondary summit P. 396m (on the right) and P. 368m (on the left). Le Muy greets us from the depths of space.

Experiencing the best of the Côte d'Azur: the east-west traverse of the main ridge of the Rocher de Roquebrune. It forms the distinctive skyline of the pretty village of Roquebrune-sur-Argens and for a few minutes captivates drivers on the Côte d'Azur motorway with the name 'Estérel'. The Rocher de Roquebrune lies at the outer limits of the Massif des Maures and with its red rocks belongs geologically to the Estérel. Mountain walkers will also be reaching their limit at this ridge walk.

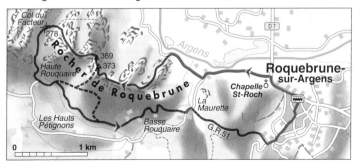

From below: silhouette of Rocher de Roquebrune which we climb from left to right.

In **Roquebrune-sur-Argens** follow the D 7 northwestwards towards the motorway. Immediately after the Chapelle St-Roch (11m) go left onto the side road which leads to L'Argens. After a sharp left hand bend you come to a fork (you can leave your car or bike nearby). Go right to the rocky north side of the Rocher de Roquebrune.

The **start** of the **east ridge walk** is at the most northern tip of the rock slabs where they meet the road for the second time, to the west of a derelict house with the sign 'Défense d'entrer'. Immediately afterwards the road bends round to the left – but at that point you have gone too far. Go up across the slabs, sometimes covered in vegetation and loose stones, southwestwards as far as the first tower. Below this you will find a cairn and the first blue markings. Go round the **first tower** by crossing a slab (somewhat exposed) and following a track right covered in dense undergrowth. You eventually reach the east ridge itself and look down its south side.

Continue through undergrowth over the ridge. There are no holds on the slab lying on the south side of the next hump of rock. You come to the ridge again and there's again vegetation. The path is indistinct, but you keep going towards the next red tower. Go round the corner at the bottom of this with the use of a cable (somewhat exposed). Afterwards you continue on the south side over some overgrown boulders. After a conspicuous red tower you come again to the east ridge and continue easily along the mostly flat ridge. Go round the next hilltop to the left and over the adjoining hilltop. Go round the north side of the following rise where there's an exposed traverse with a cable. Descend and walk to the **prominent tower** at the foot of the summit ridge.

Descent on the south side by cable: continue the descent partly on scree and traverse below the rock faces. One place is made safe with a cable. Climb up an overgrown gully into a cleft behind the large red tower. Cross the next rise below the highest point on the south side, then go over two elevations. Descend a few metres, traverse on a rock band where there's a tree trunk to help you, through a hollow to the last elevation and over this to the gap where the yellow-marked route meets from below (alternative). A few steps to the middle one of the three crosses (they stand for the painters Giotto, Grunenwald and El Greco) and you are on the highest point of the **Rocher de Roquebrune** (373m).

From the main summit go westwards down the rocks following white paint markings, white stars as well as blue paint and dots. Two places are made safe with cables. Descend into a gap and then ascend northwards. You eventually reach **P. 369m** from the southwest.

Follow the waymarkings going west over partly overgrown rocks onto a flat area where the paths divide. One white-marked path descends over the south flank down to the GR 51, but the nicer way is to go right along a white or blue marked path over rocks and through undergrowth to the col between the second and third summit. The third summit can be climbed on its east flank by ascending diagonally left. There are sections of climbing grade 1. With the help of a chain go over a steep step and then right. Finally over boulders, stepping a little to the right, up to the summit block of **P. 368m**.

Return for a few metres along the same route. Then go right and down through seemingly denser undergrowth to the **Col du Facteur** (278m). At this point all difficulties are over. Take a good path going south which is no longer so densely vegetated and even across quite open ground at times, and descend to the Bergerie Haute Roquaire where you meet the GR 51. Continue along this at the foot of the Rocher de Rouquebrune to the side road, mentioned at the start, near La Maurette (11m). Go eastwards on small roads, then on a footpath through a small valley up to a turning-place (67m) and to the first houses of Roquebrune-sur-Argens. At the point where the GR 51 turns left into an access road from private houses, it's best to stay on the road into the Quartier Ste-Anne, going past the cemetery and the memorial to the parachutist from the 15th of August, 1944 (liberation of Provence). Eventually go north into **Roquebrune-sur-Argens** centre.

24 Fort Freinet, 450m – Roches Blanches, 637m

The former Saracen stronghold and the gulf of St-Tropez from above

La Garde-Freinet – Fort Freinet – Croix des Maures – Roches Blanches – La Garde-Freinet

Location: St-Tropez (0m); compare Walk 27.
Starting point and destination: La Garde-Freinet (360m). Accessible by bus from Le Lavandou and St-Tropez [Sodetrav 70; tel: 04 94 65 21 00].
Walking times: Ascent 1¾ hours, descent 1 hour. Total time 2¾ hours.
Ascent: About 300m.
Distance: 7.5km.
Grade: Some sure-footedness and route-finding ability needed. Poorly maintained, unmarked paths.
Best time of year: All year round, except perhaps Nov., Jan. and Feb.; there's no festival in La Garde-Freinet these three months; otherwise there's always something going on – carnival, mid-summer night festival, sweet chestnut festival.
Stops and accommodation: 5 Hotels; Gîte d'Étape, tel: 04 94 43 64 63; Camping Municipal St-Eloi, tel: 04 94 43 62 40.
Alternative: Only do the round walk which takes just under an hour to the fortress and the Maures' cross. Or cycle along the tarmac road of the Crêtes (it branches off just to the north of the town campsite) to the col (568m) and in 10 min. on the path over the west ridge to Les Roches Blanches.
Places of Interest: The gulf of St-Tropez

from above.
Map: TOP St-Tropez – Ste-Maxime – Massif des Maures (3545 OT).
Tip: If there's shooting in progress (from the Ball-Trap), or motorcycling events taking place, it's best to avoid the Route des Crêtes and the fire-protected road D.F.C.I. No. 9.

The smell of flowers, bushes and sweet chestnut forests – and the smell of history. La Garde-Freinet was the main Saracen base from 889 to 975. The fortress itself, which was converted into a castle in the 15th century, goes back to a Celtic-Ligurian fortified town.

From the square with the restaurants in **La Garde-Freinet** go through the tiny streets past a small square. Go along Rue de la Croix into the uppermost street above the church and along this to a car park near the most northerly houses in this little town. Enter the wood on a broad path and you quickly reach a fork. The path to the Croix des Maures turns off left, but you go straight on, not actually on the broad path, but on a path running above it.

The path, partly hewn from the underlying rock, soon zigzags up straight to the fortress. You meet the path coming from the Croix des Maures on the left just below the fortress. Continue over rocky terrain up to the ruins of **Fort Freinet**.

Descend from the hill to the fork. Go along the link path to a col and up to the eight metre high **Croix des Maures** (437m). Going south below this you come to the next cross roads. A somewhat broader path leads back left to La Garde-Freinet (take this path on your return) and on the right there's a path on the town side of the ridge to the car park at the col (438m), where the tarmac *Route des Crètes* changes over from the east to the west side.

However you ascend along a fairly steep stony path over the ridge to a reservoir. Go gently down the gravel access road to the *Route des Crètes*. Follow it into a long bend

Picturesque respite: the Saracens once spread fear with their piracy from La Garde-Freinet.

round to the right. Now go up left without paths through bushes to an old mule path which is partly walled (you can see this from the road). This path, which at one point is only two metres above the Route des Crètes, leads to a broad col (494m). Ascend southwards on a broad path marked 'Ball Trap'. After the second sharp bend keep left and continue over the ridge, going across the motorcross slope on the left. Where the slope descends into a right hand bend, you will find a narrow path which is the only way through the undergrowth over the north ridge to the **Col des Roches Blanches** (602m, two antennae). Continue over the ridge, now on a broader path which narrows before the summit again and passes a conspicuous band of quartz. An approximately 2.5m high cairn stands on the highest point of the **Roches Blanches**.

Descend the way you came up. Two important points: firstly you must not miss the 'escape' from the mule path onto the road. The former does continue further, but gets tangled up in very prickly bushes on the col south of P. 519. Secondly choose the direct descent from the Croix des Maures to **Garde-Freinet**.

25 Chartreuse de la Verne

Sweet chestnuts, cork oaks and the Carthusian monastery of Verne

Collobrières – Plateau Lambert – Chartreuse de la Verne – Sommet de l'Argentière – (Le Grand Noyer) – Maison Rusca

The scent of stillness: peeled cork oaks above Collobrières.

One of the delightful places in the hinterland of the Côte d'Azur: Chartreuse de la Verne. You approach the monastery on foot. It was founded by Carthusian monks in 1170, destroyed by fire, plundered in the revolution, re-inhabited by an Order of monks in 1983 and is still being restored. The access on foot will have been difficult when it was constructed on this hill amongst green sweet chestnut trees.

Starting point: Collobrières (155m) on the D 14 from Pierrefeu-du-Var to Grimaud; busses from Toulon [Transvar, tel: 04 94 53 78 46].

Destination: Maison Rusca (82m) – on the IGN-map Baraque de Bargean – on the N 98 between Col de Gratteloup and La Môle; bus stop for Toulon – Le Lavandou – St-Tropez [Sodetrav tel: 04 94 12 55 00]. The *GR 90* continues to Bormes-les-Mimosas; compare Walk 26.

Walking times: Collobrières – Chartreuse de la Verne 3¾ hours, Chartreuse – Maison Rusca 2¼ hours. Total time 6 hours.

Ascent: 610m, descent 680m.

Distance: 20km.

Grade: Stamina for the descent route via Le Grand Noyer which is harder, longer, more prickly and more exciting than the fire-protected road and it also needs good route-finding ability. Mostly marked.

Best time of year: All year round; too hot in summer, the paths can also be blocked off due to the risk of fires.

Stops an accommodation: In Collobrières: Hôtel Notre Dame, tel: 04 94 48 07 13;

Auberge des Maures, tel: 04 94 48 07 10; simple campsite. Refuge des Sivadières west of the Sommet de l'Argentière: small hut, always open; take with you stove, mattress, sleeping bag and water (from the Chartreuse).

Alternative: Round walk from the Maison Rusca, descend vias La Grand Noyer and continue from the Col du Péra to the Selle de la Coulette; in total 5¼ hours.

Places of Interest: Varied vegetation up to the Plateau Lambert, cork oaks towards the Chartreuse, where there are some marvellous sweet chestnut forests, Mediterranean trees and bushes on the descent.

Map: TOP 25: Collobrières (3445 ET), Le Lavandou (3446 OT).

Tip: Opening times in winter 10-17.00, in summer 11-18.00; closed Tues., Easter, Ascension Day, Whitsun, Assumption of the Virgun Mary, Christmas and November. The Raid Nature takes place at the beginning of June in Collobrières (hiking, cycling, canyoning), in Oct. the sweet chestnut festival including organised walks.

Adjoining walks: 26, 45.

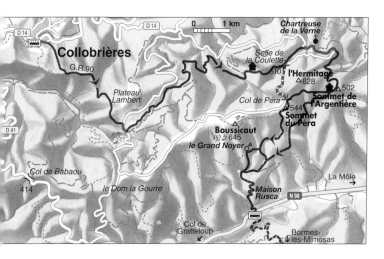

From the Pont Vieux in **Collobrières** go to the church ruins which are to the south and below the village. Go past them on the right at which point you should already be on the red and white *GR 90*. This soon leads up high over a ridge and eventually reaches the **Plateau Lambert** (474m). The path is very narrow in places, but gets wider in the second part and occasionally dips down for a short way. Go straight across the Lambert plateau and right along a little road past two menhirs (unfortunately they are not accessible). At the next crossroads leave the *GR 90* and go left along a yellow-marked gravel road northeastwards, at first gradually uphill, then downhill. After 2km do not go left over the stream. The little road now winds more or less through the wood over slopes down into the Vallon du Bousquet. Shortly after the bridge (335m) the hikers' path turns off right, climbs up through dense woods, passes a **hut** (no blankets, mattresses or wood) and reaches the little road again. Continue northeastwards. After the vast Selle de la Coulette (510m) it narrows into the path which leads straight to the **Chartreuse de la Verne** (422m).

From the monastery go along the yellow and blue marked path, at first on concrete and then narrow and on gravel – with beautiful views of the Golfe de St-Tropez – gently climbing eastwards and then westwards to the **Sommet de l'Argentière** (502m) where there's a plateau and a broad crossroads and to the northwest is hidden the Refuge des Sivadières. Two alternatives for the descent:

1) Go left onto the yellow marked fire-protected road 'Le Noyer' to the first crossroads, then left. Go next right to the reservoir. Wonderful views but monotonous and without shade. The *GR 90* comes in from the right before the reservoir.

2) Continue on the blue-marked 'piste des Sivadières' to the Col du Péra (522m); crossroads. On a path just to the south go round the Sommet du Péra (544m) to the fork. Take the left hand partly overgrown, unmarked path which goes fairly steeply southwards then westwards and finally southwards again through undergrowth and meets the widened section of a gravel path. Go left to route no. 1 (first crossroad). It's nicer to go right, to the ruins of **Le Grand Noyer** farm. This is where you meet the red and white *GR 90*. Descend through undergrowth on a path to the stream and up to the small road to the reservoir.

Now continue on the *GR 90* from the dam left above the stream on a path which soon turns into an old path with dry stone walls. Zigzag downhill and out of the valley. Where the *GR 90* goes right over the stream, stay on the left hand path. It joins the access road to a vineyard and then the N 98 with the **Maison Rusca** bus stop.

Away from the glamour: the Carthusian monastery of Verne in the middle of dense sweet chestnut forests.

26 Bormes-les-Mimosas

Well-deserved honour: premier village fleuri en France

Bormes-les-Mimosas – Notre-Dame de Constance – Bormes-les-Mimosas

Location: Le Lavandou (0m) on the D 559 which runs along the Côte des Maures. Bus Toulon – Bormes-Pin – Le Lavandou – St-Tropez – St-Raphaël [Sodetrav, tel: 04 94 12 55 00].

Starting point and destination: Bormes-les-Mimosas (157m); bus from Le Lavandou via Bormes-Pin (on the main road; from there up to Voie Romaine in the old part of the village). Also a bus from Hyères and St-Tropez.

Walking times: Village round walk and detour to the Notre-Dame, both 1 hour.

Ascent: About 250m.

Distance: 3km.

Grade: No special requirements.

Best time of year: All year round. Best in February or March when the flowers are blossoming which have given the village its name. Or in June when the Bougainvillea covers whole façades.

Stops and accommodation: Small and

charming restaurants in the village. Various hotels, eg. Grand Hôtel, tel: 04 94 71 23 72. Camping Le Bout du Monde in Cabasson south of Bormes-les-Mimosas, tel: 04 04 64 80 08; the Fort de Brégançon just next door can be visited in September on the Open Day for Historical Monuments in France.

Places of Interest: Flowers and blossoms.

Map: TOP 25: Le Lavandou – Îles de Port-Cros et du Levant (3446 ET). In the Maison de Tourisme in the Place Gambetta there's a map of the town with information about the Circuit Touristique.

Tip: On the second Sun. in Feb. there's a flower procession in Bormes-les-Mimosas, and on the 18th of August and 8th September a pilgrimage to the chapel of Saint Constance. Guided tour round the Circuit Touristique; more often in high season; dates in the tourist office.

Adjoining walk: The GR 90 goes from the Notre-Dame des Anges via Collobrières to Le Lavandou (Walks 25, 45). From Maison Rusca in the La Môle valley you go along the GR to the Col de Landon and from there on different paths via Pré de Roustan, La Pierre d'Avenon (443m), Vallon de Landon and Coste Drèche to Bormes-les-Mimosas (3 hours). From Bormes along the GR it takes 45 min. to Le Lavandou.

Parade of flowers: mimosa in February (left), bougainvillea in July (above).

A tourist walk and yet more than that. You extend the *circuit touristique* through the labyrinthine village of Bormes-les-Mimosas, full of flowers and well worth a visit, to a small hike. It takes you on a stone-paved pilgrims' trail under oak and cypress trees, olive and eucalyptus trees, pines and of course, mimosa trees, to a pilgrims' chapel from the 12th century and to the viewing point right next to it above a German bunker. The occupiers must have also admired the view of the Îles d'Or.

The signposted *circuit touristique* begins at the Mairie (town hall) of **Bormes-les-Mimosas**, which is situated at the southern side of the Place Saint-François. Follow the arrows past the Chapelle Saint-François to the **Château des Seigneurs de Fos** at the top of the village. At the castle ruins the path to the pilgrims' chapel branches off (signpost, GR 90 too). Go north for a few metres on a gravel track then turn right onto the pilgrims' path marked by six stations. It zigzags up to the **Notre-Dame de Constance** (315m).

Return on the same path to the castle and continue the round walk for tourists which leads through the winding village, built on a slope, back to the centre of **Bormes-les-Mimosas**.

Côte varoise: azure-blue coast

'The Côte d'Azur began as the paradise of the hotel trade, the Riviera of princes and the business magnates of 1900 and now provides the beaches of today's classless holiday society which has reduced the reputation of Nice and the once fashionable Saint-Tropez.' Wolfgang Koeppen's travel book 'Journeys to France', first published in 1961 has lost hardly any of its topicality and nothing of its literary delight. And it fits neatly into your beach bag. 'All French shores are people-friendly and free. The sand is not divided up into small plots, leased and sealed off in the Italian way – everyone has free access to the sea'. There's one club after another, of course, on the Plage de Pampelonne, the southern part of St-Tropez beach, but they do not go right down to the water and you can walk in front of them.

It is just that which makes walking along the Côte varoise special, the western part of the Côte d'Azur, belonging to the Département of Var. It reaches from Lecques near Saint-Cyr-sur-Mer as far as Le Trayas in the Estérel. The central point is the section from the Giens peninsula to St-Tropez with the off-shore islands of Hyères: Porquerolles, Port-Cros and Levant. The *sentier littoral* runs, section by section, along the 432km long Var coast for about 177km.

The coastal path enables you to discover the Côte d'Azur as it really was: a reddish, yellowish glimmering coast with green trees and white surf, wonderfully blue water, and equally blue sky. Moreover the *sentier littoral* gives its users a sublime feeling of outsmarting the owners of private property. Wherever possible it has been built between the private plots of land and the water.

And then as you continue walking you leave behind all the residential development. It's staggering to see how society and vegetation keep changing on the Côte varoise, due to certain sections of the coastline being saved from overdevelopment – with persistence and luck. Cap Taillat is only connected to the mainland by a sandy isthmus and is under ownership of the Conservatoire du Littoral. You can walk past it undisturbed along the 38km path around the Presqu'île de St-Tropez (Walk 28).

Cap Lardier in the nature reserve of the same name: impressive pins parasols (the umbrella pines) on the section from the Mas de Gigaro to the Plage du Brouis, which exceptionally enrich this landscape if they have not been pruned to provide maximum shade. From above they look like a sea of green fixed in windblown turmoil. Walking here is literally an immersion into a green wilderness; if the path had not been cut out of the bushes there would be no way through. And then, a few hours later at Cap Camarat, the view of the Maritime Alps suddenly opens up before you, of the snow-covered 3000ers at the southern end of the alpine arc (Walk 28).

The Plage de Pampelonne north of Cap Camaratis can be tempting with its

Savoir-vivre: on the Plage des Salins near St-Tropez a couple inform themselves about the shore path which leads to delightful secret beaches.

sometimes popular and sometimes isolated sections of beach, some where people wear bathing costumes, some where they do not. Walkers might seem out of place not only on these delightful St-Tropez beaches but also on any part of Côte d'Azur. You would do well to take off your boots and walk for an hour along the sand. On the left the smell of suncreams and sexuality, on the right the smell of sea and motorboats. If you stop off at each restaurant between the Bonne Terrasse and Plage de Tahiti you will get nowhere, but if you steadfastly resist the temptations, you will suffer from very tired thighs when you reach the continental Tahiti, just as the sunbed sellers suffer from tired upper arms at the end of the season.

Côte varoise: that is – en deux mots – naturist beaches and nature reserves. Port-Cros is even a National Park: the smallest in France and the only one in Europe which consists purely of islands and its surrounding waters. A delightful island for walking: Port-Crosis harbour is pretty, but after 10 minutes you've seen it. Walk a few steps more and you are on shady paths going past bays of which non-walkers can only dream (Walk 29). There are also lovely spots for swimming on the neighbouring island of Porquerolles (Walks 30 and 31) as well as around the Giens peninsula (Walk 32).

If you don't stay on the main beach of the Côte varoise you will come across the most beautiful and the most isolated bays, the cleanest ones with the clearest water and the best possible shelter from the wind. Only then do you lie down and take out the Koeppen book: 'At this moment a Venus, born of foam, rises up out of the waves.'

27 Cap de Saint-Tropez

The beach is always tempting: on foot instead of by yacht to the Plage de Tahiti

St-Tropez – Baie des Canebiers – Pointe de la Rabiou – Cap de St-Tropez – Plage des Salins – Pointe de Capon – Plage de Tahiti – St-Tropez

Starting point and destination: St-Tropez (0m); regular bus service Toulon – St-Tropez – St-Raphaël [Sodetrav tel: 04 94 65 21 00].

Walking times: St-Tropez – Pointe de la Rabiou 1½ hours, further to Cap de St-Tropez ¾ hour, Cap de St-Tropez – Plage de Tahiti 1¼ hours. Total time 3½ hours. 1 hour for the direct return to St-Tropez.

Ascent: About 150m.

Distance: 12km; another 4km for the return to St-Tropez.

Grade: No difficulties; only two or three slightly exposed sections where you need to keep your balance (at Pointe de Capon); two or three places where you might get wet in heavy seas (to the south of Cap St-Pierre). The *sentier littoral* is well-marked in yellow; you do not need a map, only your swimwear – and sometimes you don't even need this.

Best time of year: All year round; especially when thousands of visitors want to visit St-Tropez all on the same day.

Refreshments: Restaurants at the Baie des Canebiers, at the Plage des Salins and the Plage de Tahiti.

Accommodation: In St-Tropez: Hôtel Le Colombier, tel: 04 94 97 05 31. On the Plage de Tahiti: La Ferme d'Augustin, tel: 04 94 55 97 00, fax: 04 94 97 40 30.

Alternative: From Plage des Salins go back along the road to the Baie des Canebiers.

Places of Interest: The yachts, the seamens' cemetery, the sunbeds on the Plage de Tahiti: it would be nice to lie there one day.

Map: TOP 25: St-Tropez – Ste-Maxime – Massif des Maures (3545 OT).

Tip: Musée de l'Annonciade – the Impressionists painted scenes which walkers and tourists in November can see inside and outside the former fishing village; open daily (except Tues.) 10-12.00 and 15-19.00; closed Nov. And then into the little bookshop by the harbour – Maupassant, Colette, Sagan and guides.

Adjoining walks: 28, 45.

A very varied coast walk, watching the rich in St-Tropez harbour to see how they live on the sea and then on the *sentier littoral* to see how they live on the land. Off Tahiti beach, a real hot spot for St-Tropez beach life, walkers will find more expensive boats. They are also round Cap St-Tropez – how exclusive. And then suddenly you have the rocky coast with the strongly smelling Mediterranean vegetation.

In **St-Tropez** harbour walk to the Tour du Portalet at the beginning of the harbour mole. Descend to the sea and round the outside of the houses and Tour Vieille to the Port de Pêche and through the tiny streets of the old town up to a little road. Past the cimetière marin (seamens' cemetery) and down to the little bay Plage des Graniers. Now follow the coast path into the **Baie des Canebiers**.

Either along the sand or the small road you wind your way through the residential district of L'Estagnet, past the Batterie St-Pierre and through an archway to Cap St-Pierre. Below supporting walls which are similar to the fortified towers of St-Tropez, you come to the **Pointe de la Rabiou**. Continue along the Calanque de la Rabiou with several small bays to the Pointe de l'Ay and then along the rocky coast and over the Plage de la Moutte to **Cap de St-Tropez**.

Go past Cap des Salins to the wonderful **Plage des Salins**. At the end of the beach walk on the road for a short way until you find on the left the continuation of the *sentier littoral*. On the narrow stony path round the **Pointe de Capon** beach strollers unexpectedly break into a sweat. After the Batterie de Capon a good path leads through the pine forest to **Cap du Pinet**. The coastal path eventually reaches the **Plage de Tahiti** below the villas, where there is still some sand accessible to the public. You can even venture into one of the clubs.

There are four possible ways to return: on foot on the main road 'Chemin de la Belle Isnarde', in some beautiful woman's car, on a rich man's yacht or back along the *sentier littoral*.

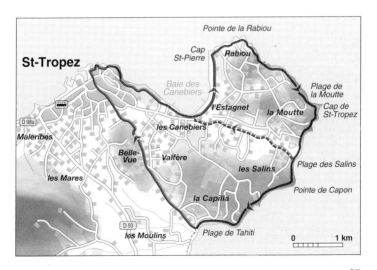

28 Cap Lardier – Cap Camarat – Cap de St-Tropez

Oh là là! Two days on the *sentier littoral* around Presqu'île de St-Tropez

Cavalaire-sur-Mer – Le Mas de Gigaro – Cap Lardier – Plage de l'Escalet – Cap Camarat – Plage de Pampelonne – Cap de St-Tropez – St-Tropez

Starting point: Cavalaire-sur-Mer (0m) on the coastal road D 559 from Le Lavandou to St-Tropez [Sodetrav buses Toulon – St-Tropez – St-Raphaël].

Destination: St-Tropez (0m); compare Walk 27.

Walking times: Cavalaire-sur-Mer – Le Mas de Gigaro 2 hours, Gigaro – Plage de l'Escalet 3 hours, Escalet – Bonne Terrasse 2¼ hours, Bonne Terrasse – Plage de Tahiti 1 hour, coastal path to St-Tropez 3½ hours. Total time 11¾ hours.

Ascent: About 750m.

Distance: 38km.

Grade: Sure-footedness for the coastal path which is exposed in places, and for the kilometre-long sandy beaches. Marked yellow.

Best time of year: All year round; restricted opportunities for refreshments and accommodation from autumn to spring.

Refreshments: Plages de Gigaro, de l'Escalet, de Pampelonne et des Salins.

Accommodation: In L'Escalet: Hôtel l'Amphore, tel: 04 94 12 90 90, fax: 04 94 79 28 22; Camping Caravaning La Cigale (with bungalows), tel: 04 94 79 22 53, fax: 04 94 79 12 05. Beim Cap Camarat: Camping Les Tournels, tel: 04 94 55 90 90. On the Plage de Tahiti and in St-Tropez: compare Walk 27.

Alternative: Start at the Allies' memorial (1944) in the east corner of the Plage du Débarquement; bus stop La-Croix-Valmer Plage; the path to St-Tropez is 45min. shorter. If you only want to visit Cap Lardier you are best to return on the *sentier littoral* to Le Mas de Gigaro (3 hours there and back); the possible return according to the map via La Bastide Blanche to the Plage du Brouisis on private property. From Cap Camarat lighthouse you can begin a good 2-hour round walk.

Places of Interest: Wild and beautifully shaped natural landscape.

Map: TOP 25: St-Tropez – Ste-Maxime – Massif des Maures (3545 OT).

Tip: In Cap Lardier nature reserve (Information: Maison de Gigaro, tel: 04 94 79 73 52) it is forbidden to light a fire or a cigarette. Cap Camarat lighthouse, April – Sept. 10-12 .00 and 14-18.00, Oct. – March 14-16.00.

Adjoining walks: 27, 45.

les Canebiers

Belle-Vue

les Salins

Pointe de la Rabiou

St-Tropez

Baie des Canebiers

l'Estagnet

Plage de la Moutte

Cap de St-Tropez

Plage des Salins

Plage de Tahiti

D 93

mpelonne

Plage de Pampelonne

Bonne Terrasse

Camarat

Cap Camarat

Hôtel

Roche Escudelier

Plage de l'Escalet

Pointe de la Douane

ge la ande

Cap Taillat

Conservatoire du Littoral

0   1 km

You would think it would be disappointing coming into St-Tropez from the wrong direction, straight into the harbour, and yet on foot. Not a bit of it! The two-day walk around the whole peninsula of St-Tropez – it's also called Presqu'île de Ramatuelle – is as fine as the sand on the kilometre long beach of Pampelonne, where the most beautiful people and motor yachts lie at anchor. But in autumn there's nothing doing in the 'Tabou' and the 'Liberty'. In contrast, however, especially at Cap Lardier at the start of the coastal trek, the *sentier littoral* can be as stimulating and unspoilt as always. The path is sometimes only a few metres above the crashing waves, just water and wind in a prickly green landscape, given an unmistakable character by the pins parasols. Walk away from the over-developed coastline through the nature reserve, the Conservatoire du Littoral du Cap Lardier, set up in 1975 and since extended. You will find it as beautiful as 'Et Dieu créa la femme', Roger Vadim's 1956 film shot on the Plage de Pampelonne with Brigitte Bardot.

In **Cavalaire-sur Mer** walk along the boulevard by the sea and descend as soon as possible to the kilometre long Plage du Débarquement and northwards along the sand or on the path to **La-Croix-Valmer Plage**. Continue right up to the furthest corner of the beach. Gently ascend and descend the *sentier littoral* mostly alongside plots of land, past three distinctive promontories to the Plage Héraclée.

Protected trees: umbrella pines shade the sentier littoral on the way to Cap Lardier.

Soon after that you will cross the stream coming from the Vallon de Valescure. Go along the Plage de Gigaro to its eastern corner called **le Mas de Gigaro** (car park).

Now you enter Cap Lardier nature reserve of the Conservatoire du Littoral; display boards (also in German) at the entrance. Go along the wonderful path over the rocky coast, round the **Pointe du Brouis**, to the Plage de Brouis.

Shortly afterwards a steep path goes above the sheer cliffs to a wooded plain (about 100m), where various paths branch off. Keeping on the west side of the summit (144m) past the ruins of a lighthouse descend to **Cap Lardier**; the vegetation gets thinner and more wind-swept. The cape itself (a 'Réservée biologique' with breeding sites for coastal birds) is closed to hikers with barriers and wire-fences

The *sentier littoral*, exposed in places, runs northeastwards above rocky bays to the edge of the Plateau de l'Huissière (vineyards) and eventually reaches the Plage de la Briande. The sandy isthmus, almost an island, of **Cap Taillat** (or Cap Cartaya) is accessible on a path behind a rocky wall. After the small Plage des Douaniers the hikers' path goes above the Pointe de la Douane and divides into two: the yellow-marked path runs across the hill, the blue one more or less follows the coast. Eventually they meet up again and go between the villas and the sea to the **Plage de l'Escalet**.

To reach the Hôtel Amphore and the La Cigale campsite, follow the beach access road for 10 minutes onto a hill (64m). After ships berths the coastal path winds through blocks of red granite into the bay of Pébriet. On the way you go past the Roche Escudelier with a memorial plaque to the secret submarine alliance in 1943/44 between the Résistance in the Massif des Maures and the French army in exile. The often narrow *sentier littoral*, with steps in places, runs as close as possible to the steep coastline. Some little cul-de-sacs lead from villas to the water. There are few urban signs around **Cap Camarat** with its pinkish-red to brownish weathered granite. Shortly afterwards the path branches off left to the lighthouse (30 minutes).

Go along the rocky coastline with its inaccessible bays and an eroded stream bed to **Bonne Terrasse**. The path is sometimes exposed and very stony. Go round the Pointe de la Bonne Terrasse to reach the southern corner of the **Plage de Pampelonne**. Walk for 4km along the sand to the **Plage de Tahiti**, possibly getting wet feet at the point where the Gros Vallet stream joins the sea. As in Walk 27 continue on the *sentier littoral* to **St-Tropez**.

Unspoilt coast: it's not far to the Plage de Pampelonne from Cap Camarat.

29 Île de Port-Cros

On great hiking paths round a national park

Port-Cros – Plage de la Palud – Baie de Port Man – Fortin de la Vigie – Pointe du Cognet – Plage du Sud – Port-Cros

Starting point and destination: Port-Cros (0m). Regular boat service all year round from Le Lavandou [Vedettes Îles d'Or, tel: 04 94 71 01 02]; in summer also from Cavalaire-sur-Mer and La Croix-Valmer-Plage to Port-Cros. Regular service to Port-Cros from Port d'Hyères [Transport Littoral Varois, tel: 04 94 58 21 81]. The harbours for departure are incorporated into the bus network [Toulon – Hyères – Le Lavandou – St-Tropez as well as town buses from Hyères – Gare Routière – Gare SNCF – La Tour Fondue; Information Sodetrav tel:0494 12 55 12]. There's also a direct weekly service from Porquerolles to Port-Cros [Le Batelier de la Rade, tel: 04 94 46 24 65].

Walking times: Path to Baie de Port Man 1½ hour, ascent to the Fortin de la Vigie 1 hour, return to Port-Cros 1¾ hours. Total time 4¼ hours.

Ascent: 550m.

Distance: 17.5km.

Grade: Some stamina and sure-footedness needed.

Best time of year: All year round.

Stops and accommodation: Various restaurants. Hôtel le Manoir d'Hélène, tel: 04 94 05 90 52.

Alternative: Île du Levant; accessible on the same boats as for Port-Cros. The non-military 10% of the island is for nudists and only fit for certain walks.

Places of Interest: a green island in blue water – the Côte d'Azur as it used to be long before it got its name.

Map: TOP 25: Le Lavandou – Parc National de Port-Cros – Corniche des Maures (3446 ET).

Tip: it is strictly forbidden to smoke, light a fire, camp or pick flowers. Visit the underwater park with the glass aquasope, tel: 04 94 05 92 22. The Fort de l'Estissac (with sea exhibition) is open from June to September.

Not only the 4.5 by 2 km large island belongs to the Port-Cros National Park, founded in 1963, but also the small Île de Bagaud, on which you are not allowed to land, but also the 1800 hectares of sea. In addition the French state has given four fifths of the Île de Porquerolles to the Parc national de Port-Cros, which manages the 275 hectares of Cap Lardier belonging to the Conservatoire du Littoral. The state-run underwater-world at Port-Cros can be viewed from the constructed *sentier sous-marin*. But walkers stay above the water surface and on land, and discover a unique and varied vegetation. There are 530 indigenous plants on the island, amongst them a few which are only found at this location. Beach pines and strawberry trees are wide-spread. The rustling of the leaves along the paths mingles with the roar of the waves.

From the harbour of **Port-Cross** northwards go along the *sentier des plantes* which leads past the inhabited Fort du Moulin and ascends the coastline to the Fort de l'Estissac (82m). Take the left of the two paths down to the **Plage de la Palud**. At the northern edge of the beach the path goes up some steps and through dense vegetation to the Col de la Galère (87m) where there's a crossroads. Continue northeastwards at first still in the dense oak wood, but soon with beautiful views of the sea, to a gap above the **Pointe de la Galère**. The path descends to the sea and follows it into the **Baie de Port Man**, a beautiful bathing place and popular anchorage.

At the eastern end of the beach cross a stabilised, rather exposed path quickly up to a little road. It leads over the Col de la Marma (121m) to the Col des quatre chemins(116m) where you meet the access road to the **Fortin de la Vigie**, the highest summit (199m) of the island (it's not possible to go into the fortress).

Return for a short way on the same path and towards the helicopter pad which you leave to the left. Soon you come to an impressive viewing point, 200m vertically above the water. Descend westwards along the steep coast as the path goes inland many times through woods; lots of uphill climbing, several paths branching off to the right and many breathtaking views of the sea. You eventually meet the turn-off to the **Pointe de Cognet**. It's worth making the detour.

Return to the *sentier littoral* which now goes past the Ancienne Batterie du Sud and reaches the Plage du Sud. The *sentier forestier* brings you safely back via the 'counterfeit money' bay into the harbour town of **Port-Cros**.

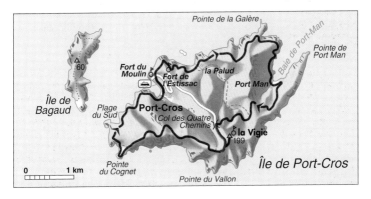

30 Île de Porquerolles – circuit culturel

Walk to cultural and botanical sights

Village – Conservatoire botanique – Phare – Fort Ste-Agathe – village

Starting point and destination: Porquerolles (0m). Reached most quickly by boat (20 min.) from La Tour Fondue [Transport Littoral Varois, tel: 04 94 58 21 81]; several daily; arrive early as the boats often depart before time. You can reach La Tour Fondue from Hyères by car or bus from the Gare Routière [Info Sodetrav, tel: 04 94 12 55 12] stopping at the Gare SNCF; to here by train from Toulon. You can also reach Porquerolles directly by boat from Toulon [Le Batelier de la Rade, tel: 04 94 46 24 65; also perhaps Transmed 2000 Monarque, tel: 04 94 92 96 82] as well as from Le Lavandou, from

Cavalaire-sur-Mer and from La-Croix-Val-mer-Plage [Les Vedettes Îles d'Or, tel: 04 94 71 01 02]; these boats usually only run in summer. That's also true for the service from Porquerolles to Port-Cros; compare Walk 29.

Walking time: 2 hours.

Ascent: 120m.

Distance: 7km.

Grade: None.

Best time of year: All year round. The season on Porquerolles lasts from mid-April to mid-October, fully occupied during Bank Holidays and in high summer. In winter – with the exception of Christmas – the village

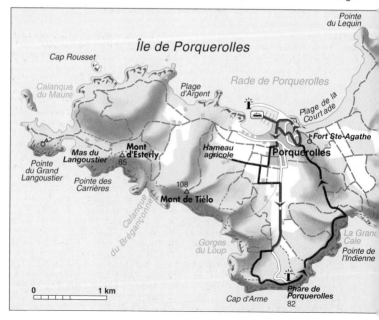

An island of dreams for cyclists: free-wheeling with rental bikes from Langoustier point.

is almost deserted.

Refreshments: In the village.

Accommodation: Auberge les Glycines (the best address in the village, comfortable rooms, inner courtyard) tel: 04 94 58 30 36; Sainte Anne (at the top of the Place d'Armes) tel: 04 94 58 30 04; Café Porquerollais (a good place to stay) tel: 04 94 12 32 70. If you want something more exclusive take a room in the Mas du Langoustier some distance from the village tel: 04 94 58 30 09. Holiday apartments.

Alternative: Cycling: the four broad paths and small roads are really inviting. Porquerolles, which is free of cars – only approved vehicles are allowed – makes a living from the renting of bikes. In high summer the approximately 1500 rental bikes are booked from midday onwards. Taking your own bike on the boat costs about as much as the rental of a normal bike. One shop which can be recommended is L'Indien at the entrance to the village; there are also children's bikes in all sizes, trailers and full suspension bikes; tel: 04 94 58 30 39.

Places of Interest: The Place d'Armes in the middle of the village, formerly the parade ground, today where the locals play boules while the tourists sit on the wall writing cards and reading *My Friend Maigret* by Georges Simenon.

Map: TOP 25: Hyères – Île de Porquerolles (3446 OT). In the Bureau d'Informations (closed at midday) at the entrance to the village there's a good map on sale for 10 FF (1:27.000) with bike and footpaths.

Tip: Phare de Porquerolles: open daily April – Nov., 10 (more precisely 11) -12.00 and 14-16.00, sometimes 17.00; operational of course in winter too. Conservatoire botanique national: you can visit the orchards (with a few exceptions) and flower gardens free of charge during the day; information centre open June – Sept. (guided tours); tel: 04 94 58 31 16. Fort Ste-Agathe: museum of marine archeology (opening times in the tourist office). Wines (all Côtes de Provence A.O.C.) from the three vineyards of Domaine de l'Île, Domaine Perzinsky and La Courtade: you can taste the wines of the last two at the vineyards; on sale in the village shops. Smoking is forbidden outside the village.

Adjoining walk: 31.

... for gourmets: blackberries from the bush.

A dream island for walkers: Porquerolles lies on the same degree of latitude as the Cape of Corsica. The lighthouse built in 1823 is the southern-most point of the coast between Menton and Marseille. It's inhabited, but you can visit it. The secret of Porquerolles is that the island has the right mix of locals and tourists. The daytime is dominated by trippers, but tranquillity returns to the village by night and strangers are made to feel like guests. If they leave early the next morning they will be alone with the pheasants and hares. The Fort Ste-Agathe, the oldest fortress on the island, dates from the 5th century. The Conservatoire botanique national has only been in existence since 1979. The French state bought the 1000 hectare wide area (that's four fifths of the island) in 1971 and presented it to Port-Cros National Park. The National Botanical Museum collects the (endangered) plants of the (French) Mediterranean amongst others and cultivates plantations with date palms, 22 different almond, 60 apricot, 100 olive, 154 fig, 200 peach trees and 50 blackberry bushes.

From the mooring on **Porquerolles** walk into the village. Go past the Place d'Armes, then turn right onto the little road towards the Plage d'Argent. After 150m turn left onto the field path to the Perzinsky vineyard. Go past it on the left to a little gravel road which, at the **Hameau agricole** (with the **Conservatoire botanique nationale**), turns into an avenue with over-arching trees. After a visit to the exhibition, where you can find out which fruits are ripe and which you are allowed to taste, return to the avenue and the little road. Continue along this to the entrance to the arborium. A board displays what is growing and where. Go straight ahead to a table under some shady trees. There are blackberry bushes on the right close-by. Go up to a path and eastwards to the avenue which leads southwards to the lighthouse. At the point where the route really begins to ascend leave it to the right towards the Gorges zu Loup, but at the next fork take the left hand footpath. This leads to the south coast and eventually joins the little access road again to the **Phare de Porquerolles** (82m).

A few metres north of the lighthouse turn onto the continuation of the south coastal path which leads high above the water to the Pointe de l'Indienne. Continue across the edge of both bays of Grand Cale. From **Grande Cale Est** (where big boulders block off the precipice) go northwards on a path lined with umbrella pines to the Carrefour des Quatre Chemins and up into the **Fort Sainte-Agathe** (57m). If you want to go straight into the village take the path beginning at the north side of the fortress. If you want to go swimming return for a short way towards the Carrefour until a path descends northwards to the Plage de la Courtade and return to **Porquerolles** harbour on the little road.

... for romantics: atmospheric evenings with hotel and Fort Ste-Agathe.

31 Île de Porquerolles – circuit naturel

Coastal trip on 'secret' paths around almost the entire island

Village – Plage d'argent – Trou des Pirates – Langoustier peninsula – Calanque de Brégançonnet – lighthouse – Calanque de l'Oustau de Dieu – Mont des Salins – beaches of Notre-Dame, Alycastre, Courtade – harbour

Starting point and destination: Porquerolles (0m); compare Walk 30.
Walking times: Porquerolles – Pointe du Grand Langoustier 1½ hours, western point – Phare de Porquerolles 1¾ hours, lighthouse – Mont des Salins 1 hour, return to Porquerolles 1¼ hours. Total time 5½ hours.
Ascent: About 600m.
Distance: 20km.
Grade: Sure-footedness required as well as keeping an eye open for the makeshift path which sometimes runs directly alongside or above the water, and sometimes through

undergrowth too. A bush knife is not necessary, just scratch-proof thighs. Marked in places.
Best time of year: All year round.
Refreshments: In the village; drinks stall on the Plage d'Argent. No springs on the way.
Accommodation: Compare Walk 30.
Places of Interest: Out on the coast: only water, wind and paths.
Map: Compare Walk 30.
Tip: Smoking outside the village is not permitted. Camping and bivouacs forbidden.
Adjoining walks: 30, 45.

An island of dreams for sailors: buy the croissants before the Mistral churns up the sea.

A dream island for hikers. Porquerolles is 7.5km long, 2 to 3km wide and thereby the largest island of the Îles d'Or, the golden Archipelago of Hyères. The north coast is flat with three delightful large beaches. The south coast is steep and sheer with up to 100m cliffs. 80km of paths and tiny roads run over the island which, like an enormous ship, is anchoring offshore from the mainland, half azure-blue, half covered in villas. On Porquerolles there is always something to do, especially if you like to while away time in every secret bay, but you will discover a lot more if you go round the island by boat. There are new yellow signposts at many of the crossroads which often have 'village' on them. So you can always find your way back into the village. However the distances given are not always reliable.

From the mooring point on **Porquerolles** walk into the village. Go past the Place d'Armes and then go right, along the little road to the **Plage d'Argent** which you can reach via the first little cul-de-sac, and across the silver sand. Go over a rocky spur into the next bay, the **Anse Bon Renaud**. Go up left at the end of this onto a broad path (*Voie à Langoustier par le bord de la mer*). Follow it for a few metres, then descend a vegetated path to the **Crique de l'Aiguadon** (small bay). Go right by the sea over sharp-edged slate on a path just to the right of the undergrowth, sometimes right through it. You come to the Crique d'Aiguade. Shortly afterwards, in calm seas, you could jump over to Cap Rousset. Stay beside the sea and go past two more bays. Shortly

... for mermaids: sandy beaches of every length and in every location await you.

after the second one, the **Calanque du Maure**, the path stops. The cliff is too steep. Immediately left of it you go through part of the wood to the **pirates' hole**. If you dare you can descend some steps through this tunnel to the sea. On the left of the entrance for the Trou des Pirates go up onto the Langoustier path. It's best to keep on this path to the Langoustier peninsula although there are plenty of others luring you away through the bushes to the shoreline, but they can get tangled up with one another. Go across the narrow isthmus **Presq'île de Langoustier**, straight ahead to the **Pointe du Grand Langoustier**.

For the return you follow the paths to the Langoustier fortress, which you can easily climb into. The path begins at the southeastern corner of the ruin and leads you back through very dense vegetation to the isthmus. Side paths turn off on the way to secret bays and finally to the Plage Noire. A few metres north of the entrance to the private Mas du Langoustier there's an unmarked path going east. It leads through the wood, comes left past some tennis courts to a crossroads. Go more or less straight on and uphill to a small quarry, then keep right to an huge empty water tank. After this take the right hand path which leads upwards like a dry stream bed. You eventually cross the approach road to the Mas de Langoustier and ascend the path towards the Pointe des Carrières and Brégançonnet. You come to the turn-off to the **Pointe des Carrières**. According to the signpost it's 0.3km to the top on a narrow path. (It's worth making the detour!). Go back to the turn-off and eastwards to the **Calanque du Brégançonnet** which you reach after descending from Mont d'Esterly (85m). From Brégançonnet bay go a short way east on the broad approach road, then turn right onto a path which zigzags up to **Mont de Tiélo**, first onto the western summit (106m, very beautiful viewing point) and then onto the main summit (108m, ruins of a watch tower).

From the summit go along the steep coast to a col. From below a wider path comes up from the Hameau agricole. First continue uphill through dense wood, then descend with some shorter ascents in between, sometimes in the wood, sometimes through six-foot-high vegetation, all the time with beautiful views of the furrowed slate coast. You reach the **Gorges du Loup** which is a short stony, moderately inclined gully descending into a rocky bay. From the waste bin by the sand, where the broad approach path comes down to the Gorges du Loup, descend southwards to a water course and up the other side to a narrow path. It leads you quickly to the **Phare de Porquerolles** (82m). On the way it's possible to make another detour to the Chevreaux cliff. A few metres north of the lighthouse turn onto the continuation of the south coastal path which leads high up above the water to the **Pointe de l'Indienne**. Continue across the edge of both bays of Grand Cale to the little road which comes from the village. Follow it for a short way, but always keep right, go round the **Pointe de l'Oustau de Diéu** and then down to the bay of the same name. From the pebble beach go inland for a short way in a cutting until a path leads right into bushes. It zigzags up to the **Mont des Salins** (127m).

Left of the building descend very steeply to a cistern at the end of a little road which comes to the inaccessible Calanque des Salins. The south coastal path ends here. The continuation over the Monts Sarranierto to the Plage de la Galère is clearly more difficult. The path is overgrown and descends steeply in places. Added to that the eastern part of the island is either in private or military hands and therefore not accessible. So, from the edge of the **Calanque des Salin**, go northwards along the edge of the Plaine de Notre-Dame to the **Plage Notre-Dame**, then westwards on a small road (do not go directly round the Pointe du Pin), until a path (easy to miss) descends to the **Plage de l'Alycastre**. From its western corner go through the undergrowth up to the approach path for **Fort Alycastre**. Go round the outside of the fortress, then turn right onto a path which goes through very dense vegetation and westwards above the cliffs. You come to the approach road to the closed Fort du Lequin and follow this until a path turns off right to the **Plage du Lequin**. Continue to the **Plage de la Courtrade**. Finally, on a path just a few metres above the water, you return to **Porquerolles** harbour.

32 Presq'île de Giens

Refreshing coastal walk where you come into close contact with the sea spray and the pines

Plage de la Badine – La Tour Fondue – Giens – Port du Niel – Pointe Escampobariou – La Madrague – Port du Niel – Giens

Starting point: La Badine bus stop (0m) on the D 97 from Hyères to La Tour Fondue, the harbour for Porquerolles; at the turn-off for the road to La Madrague. By bus from Hyères Gare Routière via Gare SNCF (to here by train from Toulon) direction La Tour Fondue/Giens Village; the buses go either to one or both stations depending on the service [Sodetrav, tel: 04 94 12 55 00].

Destination: Giens (50m); Sodetrav bus via La Badine to Hyères.

Walking times: La Badine – La Tour Fondue 1¼ hours, La Tour Fondue – Giens 1½ hours, Giens – Pointe Escampobariou – La Madrague 3 hours, La Madrague – Giens 1¼ hours. Total time 7 hours.

Ascent: 500m, descent 450m.

Distance: La Badine – La Tour Fondue 3.5km, La Tour Fondue – Giens 4.5km, Giens – Pointe Escampobariou – La Madrague 9km, La Madrague – Giens 3km. Total distance 20km.

Grade: Sure-footedness needed in some places, especially east of Pointe Escampobariou, where a cable helps you half way across on exposed section. The *sentier littoral* is good and marked yellow.

Best time of year: All year round. You might get a shower in some places when the waves are big.

Refreshments: Plage de la Badine, La Tour Fondue, Plage du Pradeau, Giens (Albatros restaurant) Port du Niel, La Madrague.

Accommodation: In Plage de la Badine: La Pinède campsite, tel: 04 94 58 22 61. In Giens: Hôtel Provençal, tel: 04 94 58 20 09; Relais Bon Accueil, tel: 04 94 58 20 58. In La Madrague: Camping Olbia, tel: 04 94 58 21 96.

Alternative: Only do parts of the walk; round walk from Giens around the western corner of the island; 4¼ hours. From Hyères old town it's worth taking a trip to Mont Fenouillet; 2½ hours.

Places of Interest: Rocks, trees, water.

Map: TOP 25: Hyères – Île de Porquerolles (3446 OT)

Tip: Tuesday market in Giens. The Pointe Escampobariou is the setting of Joseph Conrad's last novel 'Rover'.

Adjoining walks: 30 and 31.

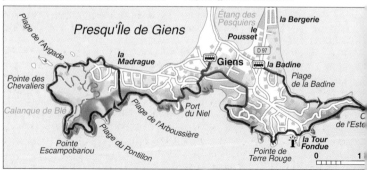

One way to go: walking is better than swimming – but there are no beaches on the west side anyway.

The Giens peninsula: a stubbornly resistant piece of the Côte d'Azur. It was once a real island and is now joined to Hyères on the mainland by just two strips of sand with a road running over each. In between there are flat pools in which they used to mine salt at one time. The *sentier littoral* runs round almost the whole island. Thanks to the bus from Hyères to La Tour Fondue where the boats moor for Pourquerolles, you can easily do the walk if you don't have a car. Either way, you still have to come back to the Plage de l'Arboussière, protected from the Mistral and over-development, from your destination of La Madrague and return on your original path to Giens village situated on the hill. But that should not bother you since this stretch of path deserves two stars, and there are two restaurants in the pretty harbour of Niel waiting to feed hungry mouths. Bon appétit!

From the bus stop **La Badine**, where there's a board displaying the coastal path, go eastwards to the Plage de la Badine and to the right. Go above some delightful pebble bays to the big Plage de la Baume. Now the path runs through dense vegetation to the ruins of a fortress. It's not possible to go near the actual Cap de l'Esterel. Go through the 'Village de vacances de famille', then sharp left down to the coast. Continue along concrete paths below the cliffs to solitary sandy bays. Eventually you go up some steps and along a roadway to **Tour Fondue**. Descend to the mooring for Pourquerolles and keep right to the continuation of the *sentier littoral*.

After the Plage du Pradau you come to the **Pointe de Terre Rouge**, the

113

A harbour: we anchor twice in Port du Niel. There are also two restaurants.

southern-most point on mainland Côte d'Azur. Continue through a lot of dense vegetation and below some villas to just before the Pointe de la Vignette, where you have to go away from the coast round the 'Renée Sabran' hospital. The coast is rugged and rocky but there are a few pretty bays for swimming. Eventually follow the hospital fence to the road which leads up to **Giens**. The *sentier littoral* does not go into the village, but turns off beforehand into the access road 'chemin du Betton' to the 'Hôtel Provençal'. Go down some steps to the coast and to the private swimming pool of the 'Hôtel Provençal' the edge of which is used for the official hikers' path – a nice feeling. Continue along a concrete path, at sea level in places, to the **Port du Niel**.

Now the route ascends roads and paths to the north of residences. The *sentier littoral* becomes wild and beautiful as it begins to descend towards the Pointe des Morts. Go above sheer cliffs through a pine forest, then descend steeply to the **Plage de l'Arboussière**. The path climbs above the Pointe de la Galère, crosses over to the Pointe du Piguet and comes down over slippery ground to the steep-sided beach, the Plage du Pontillon. Climb up to the Point du Rabat and cross the downward sloping flank (be careful by the cable) high above the surf to the **Pointe Escampobariou** with the ruins of a lighthouse to which there is a path. Return a short way on the same path, then on the west side of the Giens peninsula go up and down around the Calanque de Blé to the Pointe des Chevaliers. Continue along the less wild, but still rocky coast to the Plage de l'Aygade. Now, following the coastline exactly, you come past a private pine forest with a campsite (some of the mobile homes are right at the water's edge). The *sentier littoral* goes round the Pointe de l'Ermitage and along the road reaches the settlement of **La Madrague**. Opposite the entrance to the harbour a gravel path begins which brings you swiftly back across the peninsula to the **Plage de l'Arboussière**. Return to **Giens** via Port du Niel, but just to the west of Hotel 'Provençale' go straight up into the village.

A coast: trees, rocks and sea at Pointe des Morts. What more could you want?

Between Toulon and Marseille: sacred ridges

'They watched the streams flowing quickly through channels and dreamed about what would happen in a few months: the water would come to rest in pools and turn to ice. The ice, preserved in towers called ›glacières‹, would be transported to Toulon and Marseille. Right at the end of this dream there would be shouts of joy as the big restaurants and special hotels paid for their ice, hardened by the Mistral in December, as if it was gold. Heavy and glistening tears mixed together with the rain water and ran over their sun-burnt faces now smeared with earth; they did not hate each other any more. It was the only day in the year when they stood together at the borders of Sainte-Baume.' The competition was as fierce and cunning as the work was demanding and difficult. In 'La bastide blanche' Jean-Michel Thibaux has written a gripping novel set at the end of the 19th century about the ice men of Sainte-Baume, a range of mountains swept by the north wind inland from Toulon and Marseille. The main character is Justin Giraud from the village of Signes. His opponent is the rich Camille Roumisse from Marseille, who no longer reached for the pickaxe himself when it rained at the start of winter and the men channelled the water – and the spring water too – into pools in order for it to freeze. Since the blocks of ice melted in transport by 20 to 50%, those of them in summer who could deliver their shrinking goods fastest to the consumer, earned the most money. And so the chips were down. But Roumisse also had a desirable daughter and Justin, who was actually promised to the fiery Magali, showed her the rough paths of the Chaîne de la Sainte-Baume and more. So it can get quite hot in this novel published in 1995 about the ice of Provence.

I discovered the book in the 'Café de France' in the Place du Marché in Signes, one of the villages at the foot of Sainte-Baume. I ordered a pastis and began to read and it was so comfortable in this shady place in the middle of Signes that it needed quite on effort of will to set off very early the next morning on the 10 hour walk to Sainte-Baume (Walk 38). Below the Col des Glacières – the name says it all – there are several of these ice houses. Strictly speaking they are round holes in the earth, walled up and covered, with only a small opening above; the ice blocks cut out from the pools would be brought in through here and taken out laboriously in summer, after they had been stored in the deep down on layers of straw. The pre-industrial sights on the Col des Glacières are not directly by the path, in contrast to the famous Glacière de Gémenos which is situated at the other end of the Sainte-Baume chain. This ice cave is just 20m deep and has a diameter of 10 metres; the roof vault has fallen in in any case. It was first mentioned in 1794 and shut down in 1912 after the first factory for the production of artificial ice started business in 1898 in Hyères, the birthplace of tourism in the Côte d'Azur.

Noblesse oblige: you are only inside the Maria-Magdalena shrine of Sainte-Baume dressed in appropriate clothing.

There has been a christian pilgrim church on the north side of this mountain since the 3rd century: Le Sanctuaire de la Sainte-Marie-Madeleine. If, after visiting this church in a cave, you walk up to the chapel on the barren ridge of Sainte-Baume (Walk 37), you will see other sacred mountains; in the north the Montagne de la Sainte-Victoire, standing like a Cyclopean wall above Provence, and in the south, Cap Sicié (Walk 35) and Mont Faron. Mont Faron (Walk 33) is the local mountain of the town of Toulon and like its shipyards, its symbol too. The Gorges du Destel (Walk 34) is tucked away to the west of Toulon, but is easily reached by public transport. Fig trees grow in the cracks of smoothly polished slabs and the water mills are sometimes so high that there isn't a direct way through the bottom of the gorge any more and you have to clamber up a steep path. The view of the sea opens up again on your return along the edge of the gorge.

Sanary-sur-Mer is the secret capital of German literature according to the affectionate and clever book by Heinke Wunderlich *Spaziergänge an der Côte d'Azur der Literaten* (Literary walks on the Côte d'Azur). You should pack this travel guide into your rucksack if you are out and about between Toulon and Cassis. On the Mediterranean coast of Provence you will find bays, protected form the Mistral, where you can immerse yourself in the world of books. One such bay is the Plage de Renécros, destination of a coastal walk (Walk 36) which is easily accessed by rail. The semi-circular beach lies in Bandol and it is certainly a beautiful pace. The poet Edmond Reboul, in the 1996 April/May issue of the *Bandol Magazine*, is quoted as saying, 'Voir Bandol et y vivre, ou voir Naples et mourir'.

33 Mont Faron, 584m

Quiet hiking paths at the edge of a noisy town

Super Toulon – Tour de l'Ubac – Mont Faron – valley station for the cable car

Location: Toulon (26m), Gare SNCF.
Starting point: Bus stop in Super Toulon (141m). From the station go westwards for a short way along the main road, then on a foot bridge over the rails. Go north through a park to the number 40 bus stop Barnier to Super-Toulon. Very infrequent service on Sundays. By car follow the road to the Téléphérique and to Mont Faron; park by the cable car station.
Destination: Lavoir bus stop (about 100m) on the no. 40 route below the valley station.
Walking times: Ascent 2½ hours, descent 1½ hours. Total time 4 hours.
Ascent: 500m, Descent 540m.
Distance: 10km.
Grade: It's necessary to use your hands on the ascent over the western ridge and on the descent through the small gorge-like valley. Mostly well marked.
Best time of year: All year round; best early in the morning (better visibility). Lots of visitors on Sundays.
Refreshments: Two restaurants at the mountain station.
Alternative: Instead of the difficult descent through the small gorge-like valley do the mountain walk on the south flank of Mont Faron to the old quarry.

Places of Interest: The sea of houses in Toulon and the Mediterranean through pine trees.
Map: TOP 25: Toulon (3346 OT).
Tip: Téléphérique Mont Faron 9-12.00, 14-17.00, July/Aug. 8-20.00; closed Mon. Mémorial du Débarquement de la Provence 9.30-12.30, 14.30-18.30, closed Mon. Zoo open 14-18.00.

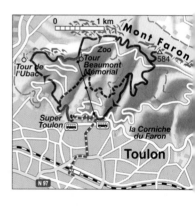

Although Mont Faron has villas and roads, a cable car and a zoo, old barracks and new antennae, hiking paths and climbing routes, it remains an amazingly green oasis at the edge of Toulon beach. At the highest point there is not even a cairn.

Take the road which branches off from the hairpin bend at the **Super Toulon** bus stop down to the bend P.125m. Go uphill and after 200m turn right onto a green marked path and climb up through the wood to the edge of a closed gravel pit. Follow the yellow markings over a flat section and cross over the road to Mont Faron. After two zigzags you come to a fork where you go left along the blue-marked former military road on the level to the **Tour de l'Ubac**.

Energetic walk at the edge of town: on the marked path above the Tour de l'Ubac.

A few metres before the tower the blue route goes off to the right ('sportif' is written up). It climbs up steep broken rocks to the antenna. Go along the small road (sometimes along the hiking path to the left of it) to the **mountain station of the cable car**, to the Mémorial du Débarquement de la Provence in the Beaumont tower and to a restaurant. Going northwards behind this past some picnic tables go eastwards on a broad path to the zoo. Continue on a broad, yellow-marked path zigzagging round to the Caserne du Centre (546m) which you leave to the left. Descend to a col (508m). Go on the gravel path to the fork in the path and left up to the summit of **Mont Faron** (584m) with the highest point lying a little away from the path.

Return to the aforementioned fork and left down to the road. Cross over the road and continue to the next fork. The route continues left, but you take the small unmarked road on the right southwestwards. Descend until you meet the hikers' path again. Go right, past a hut, until you come to a small valley (P. 397m). Now leave the road and descend a green-marked, stony path through the valley which narrows to a gorge. You must take care where the path goes briefly right and immediately descends steeply through a gully (key point, easy climbing). Continue through the bottom of the gorge to the rock face. Because of construction work in 1996 the marked route went eastwards steeply upwards again to reach the Faron road above a precipice (laboriuos detour). However we followed the previous route for a few minutes down rock steps to a bend in the road. Go along this side road to the big road. Follow this up to the right and you soon reach the valley station. Turn left to **Lavoir bus stop**.

34 Gorges du Destel

A quite different walk: uphill gorge walking without the need for a rope

Ollioules – Gorges d'Ollioules – Gorges du Destel – Ollioules

Starting point and destination: Ollioules (53m) at the southern exit of the ravine of the same name which you drive through on the N8 from Aubagne to Toulon. From Toulon (centre for buses in the Place de la Liberté below the station) with the no.12 to Ollioules, Bonnefont bus stop (the next one) or Mairie. Ollioules station is too far away.

Walking times: Ollioules – Plateau de Taillan (P. 232m) ½ hour, descent into Ollioules ravine and ascent through the whole Gorges du Destel 2½ hours, return from the entrance to the gorge to Ollioules 1½ hours. Total time 4½ hours.

Ascent: About 600m.

Distance: 10km.

Grade: Sure-footedness required; use of hands necessary over boulders and stones. The most difficult places are protected with cables. Marked almost all the way; each with different colours according to the path; the gorge route is sometimes without paths but is marked with blue paint and three small yellow dots.

Best time of year: All year round, except after heavy rainfall or thunder storms.

Stops and accommodation: In Ste-Anne d'Évenos: Auberge du Roi Bacchus, tel: 04 94 90 31 18. Two hotels in Ollioules.

Alternative: If you have a car it's better to start at the cemetery in the hamlet of Le Broussan (285m); best way to here from Ste-Anne d'Évenos (the village at the entrance to the gorge from Ollioules) is via the D 462 and D 62 direction Col du Corps de Garde. The path begins to the west of the bridge just at the entrance to the village. It is marked yellow and descends to the dry Destel stream bed. Then it's best to stay on the mountain path and return through the Gorges du Destel. Just under an hour shorter and less height difference than the route from Ollioules.

Places of Interest: The centre of the cut-flowers town of Ollioules with blossom-filled alleyways.

Map: TOP 25: Toulon (3346 OT).

Tip: The Gorge du Destel is becoming, next to Cimaï (on the D 462), one of the first class climbing areas on the Côte d'Azur; more information in *Escalades autour de Toulon*.

The windy Gorges d'Ollioules, a key section on the way from Marseille to Toulon, once had a bad reputation with travellers. Today its walls echo with the noise of people passing through. In contrast the side ravine which the Destel has carved 250m deep into the landscape is much quieter. At most you can hear the shouts of climbers on the limestone towers of the devil's castle, or of walkers who have lost their way amongst the volcanic stone blocks and the undergrowth in the bottom.

From the centre of **Ollioules** go along the *GR 51* over the Reppe river and through the Bonnefont district onto a plateau (Plateau de Taillan) to a crossroad (P. 232m). Go westwards on the path marked with yellow paint, but not marked on the map (which has 'to Évenos' written on it), fairly steeply down to the busy **Gorge d'Ollioules** (about 80m). After 300m leave this gorge and go right into the **Gorge du Destel**.

The path, fairly overgrown at first, runs through the bottom of the gorge, on the left and the right of the stream which is totally dry. On the left you come to the turn-off to Évenos. After you have gone below the limestone towers of the Château du Diable high up at the eastern edge, the gorge becomes rockier and more windy. Go over boulders and smoothly polished slabs, alternating from one bank to the other. You can use the cable or continue climbing easily in the bottom of the gorge. Continue without aid, then with a chain over a steep step. Immediately afterwards a marked path branches off right and leads up to the mountain path which you reach on the rib of rock below P. 397.

Continue upwards through the ravine until you can go no further because of a deep pool in a water-worn bowl (on the map Les Cuves du Destel). Now go right, on the orographically left flank of the ravine, very steeply climbing up with the help of a cable. After a traverse you climb a little bit more steeply back into the gorge. The view backwards to the impassable point on the ascent is worth the effort (there's an abseil ring). Continue to climb up through the gorge strewn with boulders and tree trunks. This time there's another, but shorter detour on the right hand side when your path is blocked. The markings become more and more sparse and eventually the Gorges du Destel stops.

You come onto the hikers' path which comes down from Le Broussan and crosses the Destel stream below P. 273. Follow this blue and yellow-marked mountain path out of the valley high above on the left hand side of the gorge. The path leads gradually upwards through a small side valley onto a ledge at the Vallon de Glaizas. Going up and down through this side valley you come to a rib of rock (about 360m) where the short cut joins from the bottom of the ravine.

Stay on the mountain path and shortly afterwards a path, shown on the map, branches off down to the right. You reach another spur. A little later the *GR 51* joins from the left (P. 370m). Return easily to **Ollioules**.

35 Cap Sicié – Notre-Dame du Mai, 358m

On the road-gorges to the steep coast

Fabrégas – Cap Sicié – Notre-Dame du Mai – Le Brusc Port

The concrete wastes of Toulon and its suburbs, and then the flowers and their smell on the steep slopes of Cap Sicié: gorse and bush roses, for example, and a kind of white lily on the exposed climb to the old lighthouse. In contrast to this is the new, enormous sewage purification plant which the town of Toulon is building in an isloted bay 350m below the pilgrims' chapel, Notre-Dame du Mai. The chapel stands near a TV tower on the summit of Cap Sicié which is like the bow of an immobile ship jutting out into the Mediterranean. The hikers' path descends on the west side of the viewing summit over a precipitous flank back down towards the sea. At last you can experience the freedom you neglected in the Place de la Liberté in Toulon.

From the bus terminal in **Fabrégas** go down a small road to the sea. After the Chez Daniel restaurant take a small road uphill and inland (yellow waymarkings). The hikers' path begins at the second hairpin bend. Going gently up and down over the steep flank you will see at the start several paths turning off to beaches. Where you meet a small road there's a broad path which gently ascends to the Notre Dame du Mai. However follow the small road, the former approach to the lighthouse on Cap Sicié. Although most of the supporting walls are intact the road narrows to a footpath which finally leads across the slate cliffs above the bay with one very exposed section in

Location: Toulon (28m).
Starting point: Fabrégas (23m) south of La Seyne-sur-mer. From the Place de la Liberté in Toulon with the no. 8, 189 or 198 bus to La Seyne-sur-Mer; change in Seyne-Centre onto the no. 83 bus to Fabrégas.
Destination: Le Brusc Port (0m); return by bus to Toulon, where you can change for Sanary-sur-Mer and bBndol (compare alternative). The bus stop for Bandol and Le Brusc is on Avenue Vauban just below Toulon station; this road leads down to the Place de la Liberté; you can note down the time table [Société des Transports Autocars Raynaud, tel: 04 94 93 07 45; S.A.R.C.V. Littoral Cars, tel: 04 94 74 01 35;].
Walking times: Fabrégas – Cap Sicié 1½ hours, Cap Sicié – Notre Dame du Mai 1¼ hours, Notre Dame du Mai – Le brus Port 2¼ hours. Total time 5 hours.
Ascent: About 400m.
Distance: 12km.
Grade: A very exposed path in places (but you can get round it). Marked in various colours.
Best time of year: All year round; best end April/beginning May when all the flowers are in blossom.
Refreshments: Chez Daniel in Fabrégas. Numerous restaurants and bars in Le Brusc.
Accommodation: Hotels in La Seyne-sur-mer and Six-Fours-les -Plages. In Le Brusc: Hôtel du Parc, tel: 04 94 34 00 15. Several campsites in the Forêt de Janas west of Fabrégas; Camping les Pins in the village itself, tel: 04 94 94 06 89. n Sanary-sur-Mer: Hôtel La Tour, tel: 04 94 74 10 10. In Bandol: compare Walk 36.
Alternative: Since the bus doesn't often go to Le brusc Port there are 2 possibilities to reach the crossroads in Sauviou (Plage de la Bonne Grâce) between Six-Fours-la-Plage and Sanary-sur-Mer: on the marked *sentier littoral* (1¾ hours, 5.5km) – or hitchhike. In Sauviou there are frequent services between Toulon-Sanary and Toulon-Sanary-Bandol.
Places of Interest: France for work and holiday.
Map: TOP 25: Toulon (3346 OT).
Tip: Pilgrimage to the Chapelle Notre-Dame du Mai on the 14th September.
Adjoining walks: 36: walk on the 2km long Plage de Bonne Grâce to Sanary-sur-Mer and then take the bus to Bandol; 45.

Wonderful aromas: bright April vegetation on the south flank below the chapel.

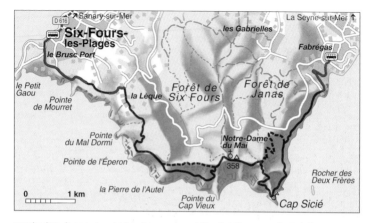

particular. A constructed path goes past the lighthouse ruins to the extreme point of **Cap Sicié**.

Return to the ruins and behind the largest of the buildings you will find the continuation of the path which zigzags steeply up some steps to a fork. The red, blue and green marked route crosses left to a gully which you then follow. At the top you come to the ruins of another lighthouse and behind that, a small road. Do not take this, but instead follow a rather overgrown path on the ridge itself to the **Notre-Dame du Mai** chapel (also called **Notre-Dame de la Garde**).

Go round the northside of the TV antenna and the path leaves the road on the following bend. Shortly afterwards you reach a fork: on the right the unexposed route along the west ridge, on the left the more adventurous route which zigzags down towards the sea, sometimes as a walled path which used to be the approach to the fortress on the Pointe du Cap Vieux. However, you follow the path westwards over the sheer flank (there's a spring on the way). After a corner you come to a wood. On the flat section (P. 148m) you need to be careful because the path descends right and soon afterwards meets a roadway. It turns into a small road which is tarmac from the **La Haute Lèque** houses onwards. Below this hamlet turn sharp left. At the end of a park go left again, along the road just above the sea and then down to the **Le Brusc** harbour, where you join one of the best coastal walks on the Côte d'Azur.

Breathtaking: the old lighthouse path gets very narrow just before Cap Sicié.

124

36 Von Saint-Cyr-sur-Mer to Bandol

From the statue of liberty along the pine-lined cliffs to the elegant swimming resort

St-Cyr-sur-Mer – La Madrague – Pointe du Défens – Port d'Alon – Bandol

Bandol is in contrast to many other tourist resorts on the Côte d'Azur even in low season. That – and the wine (the appellation d'origine contrôlée Bandol was one of the first introduced in France in 1941) – make a stay in this place on the western edge of the azure-blue coast very pleasant. In Saint-Cyr-sur-Mer you can admire an exact copy of the model for the statue of liberty erected at the entrance to New York harbour of. Of course the French one is much smaller – its height of 2.5m is the length of the just the index finger on the original.

From the station in **Saint-Cyr-sur-Mer** go southeastwards along the road into the village centre with the square of the statue of liberty. On the D 87 (signpost La Madrague, plage) go under the railway line and towards the coast. Turn left at the fork. As the road begins to go uphill you will find on the right hand side a hole in a fence and the information board 'Accès à la mer'. Go down some steps to the shore and continue to **La Madrague** harbour. The *sentier littoral* begins at the southwestern corner of the harbour. The coastal path goes up and down steps and arrives at the Pointe Grenier, which you go past on its landward side and then through a small valley. Go across the steep coast on a narrow path to the Pointe Fauconnière, then zigzag down and go over the cliffs to the Pin du Midi vineyard. After the Pointe des Trois Fours you on the right the private beach north of the **Pointe du Défens** which is developed inland, and sunbathe in the small bay after the Pointe de Terme. Reach the **Calanque du Port d'Alon** over a rocky reef. Now ascend again to a cape (taking a shortcut across the top) and then go above the rocks to the railway underpass. Go steeply up above the railway line and eventually through a pine forest high above the sea out towards the **Pointe des Engraviers**. Go down into a private bay, up to a big building and continue to the block of apartments which was built right into a bay. There's a path for walkers across the approach road. Soon after that you follow the road around the Pointe Encanet. After the Hotel Spendide go right over steps to the Anse de Renécros. Go along this almost circular beach at **Bandol**, past the Plein Large hotel, round the promontory to the harbour and along the promenade into the centre. Eventually go up along Avenue du 11 novembre until a footpath, north of the Avenue de la gare, leads straight to the station (signpost: Gare Piétons).

Starting point: Saint-Cyr-sur-Mer (24m), Gare SNCF; local trains Toulon – Marseille.
Destination: Bandol (40m), Gare SNCF; same line. Also buses Toulon – Sanary – Bandol; compare Walk 35.
Walking time: 4 hours.
Ascent: About 200m.
Distance: 14km.
Grade: Yellow-marked coastal path; stony in places, not very exposed.
Best time of year: All year round.
Refreshments: In Saint-Cyr-sur-Mer, La Madrague and Port d'Alon. In Bandol: Pizzeria La Grange, Restaurant Rascasse.
Accommodation: Hotels in St-Cyr-sur-Mer and La Madrague. In Bandol: Hôtel Plein

A strolling mile: the quayside at Bandol.

Large (the five rooms with terrace on the sea front are some of the best on the Côte d'Azur), tel: 04 94 32 23 32, fax: 04 94 29 60 12; Hotel Raimu and Hotel Coin d'Azur (tel: 04 94 29 46 53).
Alternative: Straight to the station in Bandol.
Places of Interest: Plage de Renécros in Bandol – like a private bay, but public and four different access paths; no traffic, but a few restaurants and hotels. And evening sunshine.
Map: TOP 25: Aubagne – La Ciotat (3245 ET), Toulon (3360 OT).
Tip: At the Maison des vins de Bandol, Allée Vivien, 83150 Bandol, tel: 04 94 29 45 03, you can learn everything about the famous wine.
Adjoining walks: 35, 45.

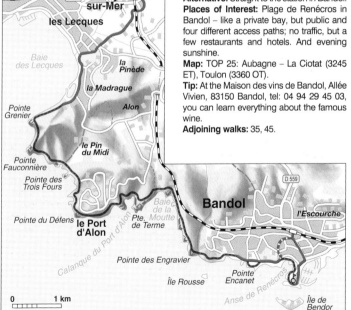

37 La Sainte-Baume:
Chapelle du Saint-Pilon, 1000m

To holy sights and an amazing viewing point

Hôtellerie de la Sainte-Baume – Grotte Sainte-Marie-Madeleine – Chapelle du Saint-Pilon – Hôtellerie

Location: Aubagne (107m).
Starting point and destination: Hôtellerie de la Sainte-Baume (668m) on the D 80 between Plan d'Aups and Nans-les-Pins north of the Sainte-Baume chain of mountains. Bus from Aubagne and Marseille (only Sat/Sun).
Walking times: Ascent 1½ hours, descent ¾ hours. Total time 2¼ hours.

Ascent: 400m
Distance: 5km.
Grade: A surprising and sometimes exposed ascent which requires sure-footedness.
Best time of year: All year round; possible black ice in winter.
Stops and accommodation: Gîte d'étape à l'Hôtellerie de la Sainte-Baume, tel: 04 42 04 54 84, fax: 04 42 62 55 56.
Alternative: Without Pas de la Cabre noticeably easier (blue); takes the same time.
Places of Interest: Maria Magdalena church in the cave; the name 'Baume' comes from the Provençal 'baumo' (grotto).
Map: TOP 25: Signes – Massif de la Sainte-Baume (3345 OT).
Tip: Ecomusée de la Sainte-Baume (local museum about the life and work around a sacred mountain), open 14-17.00 except Tues. 21st and 22nd. July pilgrimage to the church in the cave; on All Saints' Day Pèlerinage des Jardiniers.
Adjoining walks: 38; Rother walking guide *Provence*: 36.

One of the sacred places in Provence: you notice this when you go on a cold February Sunday from the Hôtellerie de la Sainte-Baume through the protected forest to the church in the cave in the vertical wall and then climb up to the St-Pilon chapel on the kilometre long Sainte-Baume ridge. A huge number of walkers and hikers traipse along the paths of the Romans and Saint Maria Magdalena, of popes and kings. There are pilgrims in sandals (and with guardian angels) who brave the path to the Pas de la Cabre which can be precipitous.

Take the path which begins east of the **Hôtellerie de la Sainte-Baume**, and goes across the flat field to the edge of the forest and to a fork. Turn right into the *Chemin du Canapet* and the *GR 9*. After a left hand bend it begins to climb up to the rock face, clinging to which are the buildings of the **Grotte Sainte-Marie-Madeleine**. The other concrete pilgrims' path joins from the

Pilgrims' destination: the St-Pilon chapel on the mountain ridge offers beautiful views.

left just below it. Eventually you go up the steps to the shrine (870m).

Go down the steps again and westwards below the rock face. The broad path soon turns into a path marked with green and red paint. After a few minutes it divides: green down to the right, red up to the left. Follow the red path under the sheer rock faces diagonally upwards on a strip which cuts across the north face of the Sainte-Baume. Shortly after the fork a path marked with red dots descends to the Grotte du Père Elie. Your path is sometimes rather exposed, but distinct and easy to walk along. You come to the cleft of the **Pas de la Cabre** (953m) where there's a cairn. Go eastwards over the ridge to the **Chapelle du Saint-Pilon** (1000m) and to the panorama guide.

Descend to the **Col du St-Pilon** (950m). Zigzag on a broad path, past the chapel for the poor of Paris, down to a fork: the concrete pilgrims' path goes left to the chapel in the cave, the fenced Chemin de Roys goes right, past the Fontaine de Nans, to a car park at the foot of the flank. Go westwards on a path which leads you back to the meadow path at the **Hôtellerie de la Sainte-Baume**.

38 La Sainte-Baume: Signal des Béguines, 1148m – Pic de Bertagne, 1042m

Wonderfully long ridge walk to on ice cave on a sunny slope

Signes – Col des Glacières – Signal des Béguines – Baou du Regage – Jouc de l'Aigle – Chapelle du St-Pilon – Pic de Bertagne – Glacière de Gémenos – Gémenos

Starting point: Signes (343m) on the D 2 in the south east of the Chaîne de la Sainte-Baume, in the département of Var; Bus from Toulon [Société des Autocars Blanc, tel: 04 94 69 08 28].

Destination: Gémenos (133m) at the western foot of the Sainte-Baume mountain chain, in the département of Bouches-du-Rhône; Bus from Cours Barthélemy in Aubagne [no. 7, not Sun. or Bank Holidays], from Marseille via Aubagne to Cuges stopping in Gémenos [no.11 of the Société varoise de transport; also on Sun. and Bank Holidays]. No direct link by bus to Signes. Taxis in Gémenos.

Walking times: Signes – Col des Glacières 3 hours, ascent to the Signal des Béguines 1 hour, descent to the Col du St-Pilon ¾ hour, via the Chapelle du St-Pilon to the Pas de la Cabre ½ hour, on to the Pic de Bertagne 2 hours, descent to the ice cave 1 hour, descent to Gémenos 1¾ hours. Total time 10 hours.

Ascent: About 1100m, 1300m descent.

Distance: 28km.

Grade: Stamina and safe walking technique necessary. Marked in several places (but sometimes faintly): follow the *GR 9* as far as the Col du St-Pilon, then the *GR 98* to below Pic de Bertagne. Take special care looking

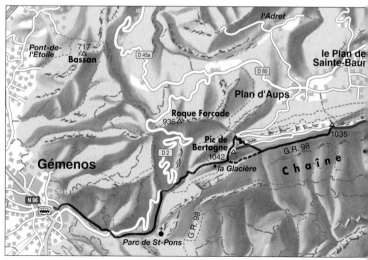

for the waymarkings and tracks on the often karstic ridge covered in bushes: you can even lose your way when the sun is shining.

The descent from the Pic de Bertagne (on the right in the picture) is easy to find, but the path is rough.

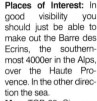

Best time of year: All year round; very hot in summer, very cold in winter (glaciers!).

Stops and accommodation: In Signes: Hôtel Acacias, tel: 04 94 90 88 07; Gîte d'étape, tel:04 94 90 88 03 (mairie); Camping des Promenades (also suitable for non-walkers), tel: 04 94 90 88 12. In Gémenos: Hôtel du Parc (in the Vallée de St-Pons), tel: 04 42 32 20 38, fax: 04 42 32 10 26. Two campsites. Just to the south of the Glacière de Gémenos is the Refuge Paul Ruat (no cooking facilities, mattresses or blankets).

Alternative: Descend directly to the glacier

southwards below the Pic de Bertagne. Or climb this summit by starting in Gémenos; a round walk is possible in the upper part.

Places of Interest: In good visibility you should just be able to make out the Barre des Ecrins, the southernmost 4000er in the Alps, over the Haute Provence. In the other direction the sea.

Map: TOP 25: Signes – Massif de la Sainte-Baume (3345 OT), Aubagne – La Ciotat (3245 ET).

Tip: A two day walk with overnight stop in the Hôtellerie de la Sainte-Baume; compare Walk 37. End June a big festival in Signes. Jour de fête de Saint-Eloi on the last Sunday in July near the Abbaye de St-Pons. There's a lot of climbing on the Sainte-Baume, especially on the Pic de Bertagne.

Adjoining walks: 37; Rother walking guide *Provence*: 35.

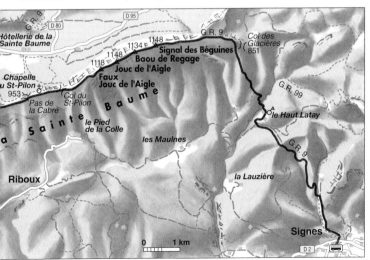

A huge reef of limestone, 12 kilometre long and 1000m high, which blocks the passage of the Mistral. You can walk for hours across this bastion if the Mistral is not blowing too strongly. The ice workers, however, were dependent on this cold wind to freeze the water. You can see where the transitory goods were produced and stored at the enormous Glacière de Gémenos (or de Bertagne), which is situated only 660 metres above the Mediterranean. Water from the nearby spring quenches your thirst and fills the drinks bottles before descending through a valley where the midday sun beats down mercilessly. Mules used to carry their precious cargo down here to Marseille.

From the Place du Marché in **Signes** go northwards through the village to the stream. Go into the valley for about 1.5km along the little road first on the west, then on the east bank. After crossing over to the west again a gravel road branches off left. The GR 9 runs mostly through the wood, descends into a

Shadowplay: even in the Provence sun and with the red and white waymarkings, the route over the 12km long ridge is not always easy to follow.

small valley and eventually reaches a stream. Go upstream until the path leaves the little road and goes left to the ruins of **Le Haut Latay**. Go behind along the mule path to the devil's bridge. On mostly overgrown terrain go under a power line up to the **Col des Glacières** (851m). You reach the pass just above the deepest point. Go westwards ascending a wooded, slightly rocky ridge. Now continue on the visibly less overgrown therefore broader ridge, partly on limestone, along a path which is not always clear to the pre-summit. From there follow a good path, which is on limestone again at the end, onto the highest point of Sainte-Baume, the **Signal des Béguines** (1148.2m) where there's a cairn.

Go along the ridge over the **Baou du Régage** (1134m) onto the **Jouc de l'Aigle** (1148m) with the Croix des Béguines. Shortly afterwards the path changes over onto the north flank, then comes back onto the ridge again, passes the **Faux Jouc de l'Aigle** (1118m) and descends eventually to the

Col du Saint-Pilon (950m) where the pilgrims' path turns off to the Hôtellerie de la Sainte-Baume (compare Walk 37). Go on a good path to the **Chapelle du Saint-Pilon** (1000m) which stands here just to the west of the highest point of the Saint-Baume ridge. You walk over several limestone pavements to the **Pas de la Cabre** (953m). The second path from the Hôtellerie comes up here (turn-off marked with a red circle and an arrow). Now the path gets narrower and without it there's no way through the overgrown limestone pavements. At the first transmitter you go left beside the fence and as soon as possible change onto the little tarmac road (where you are finally able to walk normally). Before the big transmitter go left up to the highest point on the ridge (1035m) with trees – a welcome source of shade. Now on the south side of the ridge walk over the flank first of all, then through a hollow gently descending to large pine trees and a fork. Go up right along a red marked route to the approach road for the **Pic de Bertagne** (1042m). Sadly, the western corner of the Sainte-Baume ridge is developed as well, with a white dome amongst other things. You can push the barrier open a little on the left to sneak a good view.

From the Pic de Bertagne go back for a short way on the little tarmac road, then left on the red-marked path up onto the ridge and zigzag steeply down (a rocky section) to a col with a striking wayside shrine. Going southwestwards take the left fork on a green-marked path making your way partly through undergrowth beneath the rock faces of the Pic de Bertagne. You come to a fork. On a marked path go over a wooded ridge down to the next fork on a level area. The **Glacière de Gémenos** (660m) lies hidden in the bushes just to the right of the path. On the slope there's a shady place with a spring. Continue descending west on the blue-marked route – sometimes on uneven paths, sometimes on the broad mule path on which the ice was transported – to the D 2.

Follow it for a short way until the blue-marked path turns off left on a right hand bend. Go through undergrowth on a mule path which turns into a little gravel road: the Allée des Platières of the **Saint-Pons nature park**. You come to the Abbaye de Saint-Pons in the middle of plane trees and cedars. At the access bridge to the Cistercian abbey you will find a path which goes along the right hand bank of the stream. At the moulin à blé you change over onto the left bank. Cross over the D 2 at the exit to the car park, follow the Le Fauge stream for a short way and then go over the bridge to the right. Cross over a meadow, go round the back of a carpenter's and out of the valley on a gravel path, ignoring the sign 'Danger Eboulement – Passage interdit'. At the open air theatre descend left onto the road and into **Gémenos** – and order a ice-cold sirop de menthe in the 'Idéal' bar.

Calanques: mountains of the sea

'Sometimes I set off for a stroll into the Calanques, Sormiou, Morgiou, Sugiton, En-Vau. Hour-long walks with my rucksack. I sweated, gasped for breath. That kept me in shape. It softened my doubts, my fears, my anxieties. Their beauty always reconciled me to the world. It is true that the Calanques are beautiful. You don't just have to say so, you have to visit them. But you can only go on foot or by boat.' This is how, in the moving political thriller *Chourmo* from 1996, the Marseille writer Jean-Claude Izzo had his hero Fabio Montale describe his trips into the limestone wilderness between the second biggest town in France and the Mediterranen.

Les Calanques: this word has an almost magical ring for the French. Un sanctuaire naturel (a natural shrine): 20 kilometres long, 4km wide, over 20 bays (Calanque means bay). Whipped by the Mistral, scorched by the sun. This north wind blows 140 days a year, sometimes so strongly that you can no longer stand up straight on the local mountain of Marseille (Walk 44). Only on a few days of the year does the sun not shine at all and it only occasionally rains: the Calanques is the driest region in France. 'Un parfum de sauvagerie, mélange de thym, de bruyère et d'air marin' (the scent of the wilderness, a mixture of thyme, heather and sea breeze): that's how the Calanques smelt for François Labande whose main occupation was a Maths teacher at a grammar school in the socially difficult northern suburbs of Marseille, and whose secondary occupations were environment activist, writer and author of guide books.

About 150 km of red, blue, yellow, green, brown or black marked hikers' paths as well as other unmarked paths make the fractured landscape accessible, where there are not many flat areas, only rock faces and stone edges, ridges and gullies, mountains and bays. Many paths have names like for example the black-marked *Sentier du Président* between La Madrague and Callelongue; it was constructed by the 'Société des excursionnistes marseillais' as one of the first hikers' paths in these mountains by the sea. Passionate walkers founded their organisation on Sunday, the 28th March, 1897, at the foot of the Pic de Bertagne, the south summit of the Sainte-Baume ridge in the shadow of the famous Gémenos glacier (Walk 38).The 'excurs' marseillais' protest against the destruction of their – and our – country, sometimes in vain, for example, in the Calanque de Port-Miou with the gaping wound of an enormous quarry. Often, though, with success against the project for the cable car up to the Sommet de Marseilleveyre, for example, and against the planned coast road from Marseille to Cassis. Not least, thanks to their support, the Calanques were declared a sîte protégé in 1975. And the 'Société des excursionnistes marseillais' was also present at the demonstration organised by the international environment organisation Mountain Wilderness on the first of November 1997 in the Calanque d'En Vau.

Au bout de souffle: the Pas Edgar Garrigue requires full commitment before the almost 12 hour crossing of the Calanques is over.

For several hours about 100 people blocked the entrance to the bay over which they hung a banner 'PROTEGEONS LES CALANQUES'. The Calanques are supposed to be more strongly protected having received the status of a National Park. François Labande, founding member, guarantor and former general secretary of Mountain Wilderness, has put together a 6 point plan for the rescue of the Calanques from excessive use: 1) no more boat traffic into the bays of the Calanques (especially valid for En Vau); 2) the blocking of the approach roads to Sormiou and Morgiou for tourist traffic (actually it was already forbidden); those with a justification like fishermen (Morgiou is always inhabited), holiday home owners, restaurant owners, fire brigade, rescue services etc. are still allowed entry; 3) the existing camping ban is to be upheld (but bivouacs are still allowed); 4) the building of campsites at the edge of the Calanques, in Port-Miou (in the disused quarry), at the Col de la Gardiole, in Callelongue; 5) the construction of a Gîte d'étape in Luminy, perhaps also in Sormiou; 6) the conversion of a building into a 'house of the Calanques' in Morgiou. These are good suggestions for those who are walking, onto a very special cape, for example.

Cap Morgiou is like a petrified ship on which people landed in the past. Some 20 000 year old drawings have been discovered in a cave only accessible from the water (the Calanques has been sinking over the course of time). At the furthest tip you can see the ruins of a fort built in 1616. A fortified wall at the top used to block off the approach to Cape (Walk 41). And then there's a solitary pine tree right at the edge of the Calanque de la Triperie surrounded by vertical walls. Between the windswept branches there's a board with the following request: 'Ami grimpeur. La Nature est fragile. Respecte-la.' That's valid for walkers too.

39 Calanque d'En Vau

Famous, magnificent – and far too steep for pure beach walkers

Cassis – Port-Miou – Vallon de Cadeïron – Calanque d'En Vau – Plateau de Cadeïron – Cassis

Starting point and destination: Cassis (0m) on the D 559 Marseille – La Ciotat. The station for the Marseille St-Charles – Toulon line is unfortunately 4km away from the harbour; a good 40 min. on foot along the road or 40 FF by taxi which you can also take as far as Port-Miou (tel: 04 42 01 78 96). Several bus services daily from Marseille and Toulon.

Walking times: 1½ hours each way. Total time 3 hours.

Ascent: 360m.

Distance: 9km.

Grade: In fact the walk should be graded black as the direct ascent out of En Vau bay onto the Cadeïron plateau requires some easy climbing. And the rock there is polished from use. Well marked.

Best time of year: All year round.

Refreshments: Many fish restaurants at the harbour.

Accommodation: In Cassis: Hôtel Le Clos des Arômes in the old town with a very beautiful garden (cars driving past right outside), substantial breakfast, tel: 04 42 01 71 84, fax: 04 42 01 31 76; Hôtel Grand Jardin, quiet, a short way from the harbour, tel: 04 42 01 70 10, fax: 04 42 01 33 75; Camping Cigales, tel: 04 42 01 07 34. En route: Auberge de Jeunesse La Fontasse lies about half way from Cassis to En Vau, but 1.5km from the coast, tel: 04 42 01 02 72; Refuge-bivouac du Piolet, always open, not hut with 10 places on the side path from the Plateau de Cadeïron to the Pointe d'En Vau, no water or equipment.

Alternative: Return through the Vallon d'En Vau (a bit easier).

Places of Interest: Climbers on the sheer rock faces and pinnacles.

Map: IGN 1:15 000: Les Calanques de Marseille à Cassis (3615).

Tip: Climbing and walking guides as well as maps in the Maison de la Presse in Cassis.

Adjoining walks: 40, 42, 43, 45; Rother walking guide *Provence*: 38, 39.

The excursion boats wait in Cassis fishing harbour to ferry tourists over to the bays of the Calanques. As you clamber over the harbour wall with your

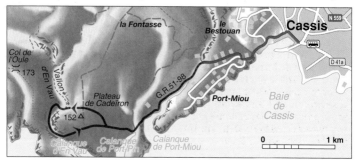

The sea: Calanque d'En Vau is very tempting. Perhaps swimming is better than walking after all.

rucksack on your back, one of the boatmen invites you to get on board. 'Non merci' – you want to walk. 'C'est bong pour les jambes', he says, laughing, in the local Provençal accent.

Go along **Cassis** harbour until you are forced to switch over to the road behind. Continue along here, following the Calanques signposts (and the red and white markings for the *GR 51-98*) to **Calanque de Port-Miou** (30 minutes from Cassis); signposts, car park, harbour. The hikers' path leads along the enormous quarry on the right hand side of Port-Miou bay and goes across a col into the **Calanque de Port-Pin**. Now take the green marked path through the **Vallon de Cadeïron** to another col (144m) where you cross a broad path. Zigzag down the scree into the ravine-like **Vallon d'En Vau**. Walk out towards the most famous bay of the Calanques.

Begin your return at the eastern corner of **Calanque d'En Vau**. The red and white and black marked path climbs back and forth up over the very steep, wooded and mostly rocky slope onto the **Plateau de Cadeïron** (134m) with some points of exposure and where you need to use your hands. It's then an easy walk across the plateau and down into the **Calanque de Port-Pin**. Walk the same way back to **Cassis**.

40 Mont Puget, 564m

Breathtaking views from the highest summit of the Calanques

Université de Luminy – Col de Sugiton – Brèche Guillemin – Mont Puget – Col de la Chandelle – Col de Sugiton – Luminy

Starting point and destination: Université de Luminy (135m); no. 21 bus from the Centre Bourse a little way north of the lower Canebière, the road from Marseille which begins at the harbour Marseille. The no. 21 has the most frequent time-table in Marseille; about 1 hour journey from the centre to the entrance into the Calanques. There are signs for parking in Luminy.

Walking times: Ascent 1½ hours, descent 2 hours. Total time 3½ hours.

Ascent: 450m.

Distance: 10,5km.

Grade: Sure-footedness is essential; the ascent through the Guillemin gully is exposed.

Best time of year: All year round, too (hot) in summer.

Refreshments: Drinks stall in Luminy.

Accommodation: Compare Walk 42.

Alternative: If you want to swim follow the *GR 51-98* into the Calanque de Sugiton and climb straight up through the Vallon de Sugiton (compare Walk 41). 1 hour longer.

Places of Interest: La Grande Candelle with the Arête de Marseille: a white edge in front of a deep blue background.

Map: IGN 1:15 000: Les Calanques de Marseille à Cassis (3615).

Tip: The Librairie de la Bourse-Freizet, 'la maison des cartes', at Rue Paradis 8 in Marseille (tel: 04 91 33 63 06) has a very large selection of guides and maps; the no. 21 Luminy bus stops close-by.

Adjoining walks: 41, 42, 45.

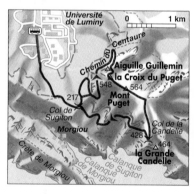

A remarkable summit walk in the eastern part of the Calanques, the Massif du Puget. The amazing thing is that the paths up to the last point are not marked. If, like me, you are alone on this walk in fog and rain, you will suddenly feel you have been transported into high mountains. On the descent you will pass the Grande Candelle, the big candle (454m). Only climbers should venture onto this pinnacle, the most beautiful in the Calanques – the normal route from the Col de la Candelle has an exposed section of grade III, called the 'mauvais pas'.

From **Luminy** bus terminus go southwards to the entrance into the protected area of the Calanques (information board). Along a small gravel road, mostly in the shade, go up to the **Col de Sugiton** (217m). Turn left onto a gravel path which leads up round two hairpin bends onto the band of rock above

The pinnacle: the Grande Candelle with its wonderfully sharp Marseille ridge. If you want to reach the top you will need to tighten your shoe laces.

the Falaises de Luminy; after the fork on the Col de Sugiton you can take a shortcut from the first bend on a path which turns off east. Follow the **Chemin du Centaure** along the curved band on the west flank of Mont Puget and arrive at a barrier. At the next promontory but one, before the mountain path comes onto the north side, a path branches off sharply right and goes into a gully to the left of the Aiguille Guillemin pinnacle. Climb up through here on exposed rock to the ridge where the path divides. On the left the *Sentier Frager* crosses over the north flank of Mont Puget, on the right a small track leads to the **Croix du Puget** (548m); views down onto the huge Luminy university campus. Without any paths go eastwards down onto a col and over the pre-summit onto the highest point (cairn) of **Mont Puget**. From the summit go over the broad east ridge onto a col where you meet marked paths again. Follow the green-marked path, later also marked yellow, over a stony flank, then over the ridge above the Vallon de la Candelle into the **Col de la Candelle** (428m). On the *GR 51-98* go over the south flank of Mont Puget through cirques and round many promontories (the reason for the path being called **'Sentier des Treize Contours'**). Finally descend steeply, either left through the rocks (rochers) or right over scree (éboulis). You are soon on a broad path, from which the GR turns off left, to the Col de Sugiton. It's a comfortable 20 minute walk back to **Luminy**.

41 Cap Morgiou

A horizontal white summit projecting with a sheer drop into the sea

Luminy – Col de Sugiton – Calanque de Sugiton – Morgiou – Cap Morgiou – Sormiou – Col des Baumettes – Les Baumettes

Starting point: Université de Luminy (135m); compare Walk 40.

Destination: Les Baumettes (96m) at the southern edge of Marseille; bus terminus for the no. 22 which starts in Métro Rond Point du Prado; to here on the red underground line from the Gare St-Charles.

Walking times: Luminy – Sugiton ¾ hours, Sugiton – Morgiou ½ hour, Morgiou – Cap Morgiou ¾ hour, Cap Morgiou – Sormiou 1½ hours, Sormiou – Les Baumettes ¾ hours. Total time 4¼ hours.

Ascent: 600m, descent 640m.

Distance: 12km.

Grade: At the border it could be graded black. Sure-footedness and a head for heights are a must; a few easy sections of climbing as you go round Cap Sugiton. Marked except in the Vallon de Sugiton.

Best time of year: All year round, too hot in summer.

Stops and accommodation: Compare Walk 42.

Alternative: There are two possibilities for the return to Luminy: from the Carrefour on the Crête de Morgiou either continue straight over the ridge to the fork above the Col supérieur de Morgiou – or go the 'long way' round via Sormiou. Both go northwards towards Mont de Luminy, over the east ridge

as far as the Col des Escampons and northwards to Luminy.

Places of Interest: The trio – Sugiton (very narrow beach), Morgiou (idyllic fishing village) and Sormiou (the biggest Calanque).

Map: IGN 1:15 000: Les Calanques de Marseille à Cassis (3615).

Tip: Don't forget your swimwear.

Adjoining walks: 40, 42, 43, 45.

Cap Morgiou is one of the idyllic places in the Calanques. If you stand right at the edge, another few steps further than the last yellow flowers, you will have the whole world at your back – just the sound of the waves crashing against the cliff 20m below, seagulls screeching, a boat chugging past. The view goes eastwards to the Bec de l'Aigle at La Ciotat, westwards to the Île Maire before Les Goudes – the whole of the Calanques coast.

From **Luminy** bus stop go southwards to the entrance into the protected area of the Calanques (information board). Along a small gravel road, mostly in the shade, go up to the Col de Sugiton (217m). Go a few metres right, then

The cape: the path runs out at Cap Morgiou, but the longing for the island remains.

left onto an unmarked path which descends quite steeply into the Vallon de Sugiton and to a small road, concrete at first and then gravel. Go along here out of the valley to the point where it leads over to the left. Now on an unmarked path descend quite steeply into the **Calanque de Sugiton** (0m) finally meeting the marked path again (*GR 51-98*). Go southwards over a steep ledge (metal ladder) and over the flank onto the ridge (about 45m) at the foot of the south ridge of the Aiguille de Sugiton. The rest of the path to Morgiou has a few really difficult and exposed places, especially at the start, an 8m high crack which you have to climb under. Go along the right hand side of **Morgiou** bay to the edge of the water and climb up right over a steep ledge (Le Pas du Renard) towards some huts. The path goes through the Corniche de Renard to the **Col du Renard** (86m).

You leave the GR at this point and follow the blue-marked path to **Cap Morgiou** (20m), on your way going through the walls of on old fortress, then over a plateau covered in bushes and eventually round the semi-circular Calanque de la Triperie up to the furthest tip. Return to the **Col du Renard**, steeply up over rock ledges to the Sommet du Cancéou (221m), the foremost summit of the **Crête de Morgiou**.

Follow the path along the ridge, sometimes to the right on the slope as well, as far as the crossroads Le Carrefour (219m); a direct path from Morgiou joins here. Follow the GR left, crossing below the walls of the Canapé de Sormiou onto a projection, and then north of this steeply downwards to the harbour and **Sormiou** bay (0m). Go up the eastern side of the Vallon de Sormiou onto the **Col de Baumettes** (178m). Leave the GR here and it's a fast descent to **Les Baumettes**.

42 The classic walk across the Calanques

The path of paths: *GR of the balcons de la Cote d'azur* from Cassis to Marseille

Cassis – En Vau – Devenson – Col de la Candelle – Sugiton – Morgiou – Sormiou – Col des Baumettes – Col de Cortiou – Sentier de la Douane – Callelongue – Sentier du Président – La Madrague de Montredon

Starting point: Cassis (0m); compare Walk 39.
Destination: La Madrague de Montredon (20m); compare Walk 44; last bus at 21.30. You can finish the walk in Callelongue (0m) if you want to; last bus to La Madrague at 19.30 (15 min. earlier on Sundays and Bank Holidays).
Walking times: Cassis – Calanque d'En Vau 1½ hours, En Vau – eastern summit Falaises du Devenson 1¼ hours, Devenson – Col de la Candelle 1¼ hours, descent to Sugiton 1¼ hours, Sugiton – Morgiou ½ hours, Morgiou – Sormiou 1½ hours, Sormiou – Col de Cortiou 1 hour, Col de Cortiou – Callelongue 2 hours, Callelongue – La Madrague 1¼ hours. Total time 11½ hours.
Ascent: 1600m. 850m to Morgiou; about 200m between Callelongue and Madrague.
Distance: 32.5km. 16km to Morgiou (2km onto Cap Morgiou from there); 4km between Callelongue and La Madrague.
Grade: The path is long, frequently stony, exposed in places, marked red and white throughout. Be careful not to go wrong: this last part of the *GR 51* is technically the most difficult. Where other places have cables and ladders to help you across, you will find in the Calanques that such help is only provided at the most difficult sections.
Best time of year: All year round, except high summer (too hot).
Refreshments: Restaurants in Morgiou (Nautic Bar, tel: 04 91 40 06 37), Sormiou, Calanque de Marseilleveyre and Callelongue.

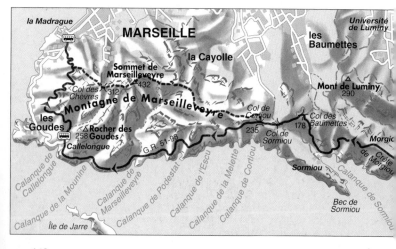

Accommodation: In Cassis: compare Walk 39. In Marseille-Montredon: compare Walk 44. No accommodation en route; three possibilities: 1) Day walk. 2) Take a break in Luminy and take the no. 21 bus to Marseille (compare Walk 40); stay overnight, eg. in the Hôtel Le Corbusier in the Cité Radieuse, 280 Boulevard Michelet (bus stops immediately in front), tel: 04 91 77 18 15, fax: 04 91 71 09 93; resume the coastal trek in Luminy the next day. 3) Camping in the Calanques is forbidden, but you are allowed to bivouac on the way. A nice little spot is Cap Morgiou (compare Walk 41); so you could have dinner in Morgiou (check beforehand to see if the restaurant is open) and have breakfast in Sormiou.

Alternative: The crossing of the Calanques is shorter and a bit easier over the ridge behind the fjord-like coastline: Cassis – Col de la Gardiole – Crête de l'Estret – along Mont Puget (crossroads 528m; it's worth making the detour to the summit) – Col de la Candelle – Col de Sugiton – Crête des Escampons – Col des Escourtines – Col de Cortiou – Tête de l'Homme – Col de la Selle – Sommet de Marseilleveyre – Sommet de Béouveyre – La Madrague. 8 hours, 1200m ascent and descent, 23.5km.

Places of Interest: A unique, hardly spoilt-mediterranean coast.

Map: IGN 1:15 000: Les Calanques de Marseille à Cassis (3615).

Tip: Take enough fluids with you.

Adjoining walks: 39-41, 43-45.

There are three hikes which the French should have done once in their life: a stroll in the Jardin de Luxembourg (or the climb up the Eiffel tower), the walk round Montblanc and the walk across the Calanques. Town, mountains and sea. Red, white, and blue. Vive la France!

Go from **Cassis** as in Walk 39 to the **Calanque d'En Vau** (0m), then through the ravine-like Vallon d'En Vau as far as the fork in the valley and westwards up to the **Col de l'Oule** (173m). Descend diagonally into the Vallon de l'Oule and down towards the sea to a fork in the path (38m). Ascend steeply up to the Col de l'Eissadon and on an exposed path to the eastern peak of the **Falaises du Devenson**: breathtaking views.

Walk along the cliffs (in contrast to the IGN map, the hikers' path keeps going over the ridge) via the **Col du Devenson** and the highest point (318m) of the

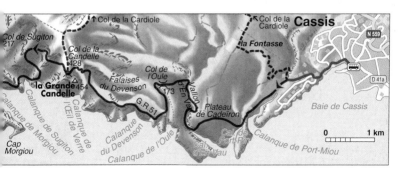

The bay: Calanque de Marseilleveyre – if you're lucky the bar will be open.

Falaises du Devenson to the **Col des Charbonniers** (242m). The path climbs northwards, goes above the Val Vierge and goes back a long way into the Vallon de la Candelle below Cap Gros, before a short descent to the **Col de la Candelle** (428m. Another direct route to this col is marked as the *GR* on the IGN map and is a bit shorter).

Continue along the *Sentier des Treize Contours*, described in Walk 45, as far as the broad path which comes from the Col de Sugiton (30 minutes from here to Luminy). Turn sharp left to the Falaise des Toits over the steep Couloir de la Cisampe and the 3m high vertical Pas des Toits. Now descend without any other difficulties to the **Calanque de Sugiton** (0m).

Follow the route described in Walk 41 – but do not bother with the detour to Cap Morgiou – via **Morgiou** (0m), **Crête de Morgiou** (221m) and **Sormiou** (0m) to the **Col des Baumettes** (178m). Go westwards via the **Col de Sormiou** to the **Col de Cortiou** (235m). Follow the *Sentier de la Douane* (former coastal path for custom officials) which bends round the flank dropping down to the sea with the deeply eroded Cirque des Walkyries, Vallon de Podestat and Vallon des Querons. From the **Calanque de Marseilleveyre** (0m) walk close to the sea with an evident climb up to 60m, to the village of **Callelongue** (0m).

Go into the valley onto the *Sentier du Président* which winds its way high above the coast across the downward sloping, deeply furrowed western flank of the Montagne de Marseilleveyre. The most difficult point is the Pas Edgar Garrigue below the Col du Brés (141m). Through the wildly romantic Vallons de la Garenne et du Piadon you come to the Crête de l'Escalette

(138m). Descend onto the road and go right to the bus stop in the village of **La Madrague de Montredon**.

The rock face: the Falaises du Devenson are 300m high – you can walk over them.

43 Crossing of the Calanques par le bord de mer

The definitive walk along the shore for summit seekers

Callelongue – Podestat – Escu – Melette – Triperie – Pierres tombées – Œil de Verre – (Devenson – Eissadon –) Oule – Port-Pin – Cassis

Starting point: Callelongue (0m), compare Walk 44.

Destination: Cassis (0m); compare Walk 39.

Walking times: Callelongue – Podestat 1 hour, Podestat – Escu ½ hour, Escu – Melette ½ hour, Melette – Sormiou 1 hour, Sormiou – Triperie 1½ hours, Triperie – Morgiou ¾ hour, Morgiou – Sugiton – Pierres tombées ¾ hour, Pierres tombées – Œil de Verre 1 hour, Œil de Verre – Col de Devenson 1¾ hours, Devenson – Oule ¾ hour, Oule – En Vau 1¼ hours, En Vau – Cassis 1½ hours. Total time a good 12 hours. – a long day.

Ascent: 1600m.

Distance: 35km.

Grade: The most difficult and the longest walk in this guide.

Best time of year: Too hot in summer, days too short in winter.

Stops and Accommodation: Compare Walk 42.

Alternative: Just under 11 hours without the detour to the 3 bays. The walk can be interrupted in several places; compare Walks 41 and 42.

Places of Interest: 19 calanques (rocky inlets) in the Calanques.

Map: IGN 1:15 000: Les Calanques de Marseille à Cassis (3615).

Tip: Enough water.

Adjoining walks: 39, 41, 42, 44, 45.

If you are already stumbling as you come down the steps from the Marseille Saint-Charles station, get tired legs on the walk over the Canebière to the Vieux Port, lose your way in the hustle and bustle of the Panier, become seasick on the ferry across the old harbour and become dizzy as you go up to the Notre-Dame de la Garde high up on a hill, you should content yourself

with a pastis in one of the fishermen's bars in Callelongue. Anyone else, should they be mountain walkers, can attempt this walk. But please not on 'le Quatorze Juillet'. Even if you walk as close as you can to the water's edge, often without shade, you will find few places for a swim.

From the **Calanque de Callelongue** (1) go along the *Sentier de la Douane* (and the *GR 51-98*) via the **Calanque de la Mounine** (2) into the **Calanque de Marseilleveyre** (3) – you can go straight down to the beach bar. Above the **Calanque des Queyrons** (4) go onto a promontory where you can see down into the **Calanque de Podestat** (5). Now along an unmarked path, stabilised in places, down to the bay and steeply up the other side (sections of easy climbing, but if you are unsure you can abandon this more exposed route). Shortly afterwards leave the normal coastal path and descend the green Route No. 5 to the Corniche du Pêcheur. A few areas of broken rock, then a chillingly beautiful traverse below and above overhangs with one very exposed section (chain). Descend a steep step protected with a cable (Pas du Bénitier). The detour, marked with green dots, soon branches off right down to the **Calanque de l'Escu** (6); the ruins of the grotto below is one of the most remarkable constructions between Marseille and Menton.

Return to the green route. Continue through the Bois des Walkyries to the **Calanque de la Melette** (7), but stop 20m above the water. As you ascend to the Col de Cortiou you come past a grotto and the unmarked turn-off to the Calanque de Cortiou. Do not go down to this bay – this is where the sewage from Marseille flows into the sea. From the Col de Cortiou go along the GR to the Col de Sormiou, then on footpaths, crossing over the road a few times, down to the **Calanque de Sormiou** (8).

Proceed as in Walk 41 to the **Calanque de la Triperie** (9) at Cap Morgiou and through the **Calanque de Morgiou** (10) into the **Calanque de Sugiton** (11).

Follow the marked path to above the eastern corner of the bay and then down the unmarked path to the right to the **Calanque des Pierres-Tombées**

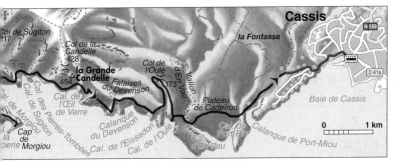

The rock step: the Pas du Bénitier is protected with cables – an exception, not the rule.

(12), where you can take off all your clothes for a swim. Go along the beach towards the island of rocks of Tonneau. Keeping left through a gully, then over a short vertical ledge, you eventually come to an easier red-marked path (Route No. 6). It leads underneath the Walk de Pise to the **Calanque de l'Œil de Verre** (13), formed by large boulders, also called Calanque de Saint-Jean-de-Dieu. The Grande Candelle towers up above to its dizzy heights.

There's a short climb, made safe with a chain, through the Val Vierge, with the Pas du Rocher Club and the Pas de l'Œil de Verre causing some excitement. And perhaps even an adder as well. The green Route No. 9 branches off right (the path going through the Val Vierge, climbing out through the devil's chimney or the Cheminée du C.A.F. demands some alpine experience, as does the whole walk). Descend across the western face of the Falaises du Devenson to the Aiguille du Devenson. Behind it, the brown-marked Route No. 6 comes in through the Petit Couloir. The detour on the very exposed, clearly difficult route straight through the Corniche Paretti into the **Calanque du Devenson** is optional.

Follow the brown route, at the start of which you have to go hand over hand along a cable, up to the Col du Devenson. From the Col du Devenson go on the *GR 51-98* over the eastern Falaises du Devenson to the Col de l'Eissadon. The tricky, steep descent to the **Calanque de l'Eissadon** (15) is up to you. But later on you shouldn't miss the detour going out to the **Calanque de l'Oule** (16) – you need to jump 10m to get into the water. Don't forget your rubber dinghy though, because there's no way back onto the rocks.

Go up the valley through the Vallon de l'Oule onto the Col de l'Oule and on the blue-marked No. 2 path over the ridge to the Belvédère d'En Vau. A direct climb out of the Oule valley is possible: from the turn-off to the Calanque de l'Oule follow tracks, in dense vegetation at first, through a gully, over a rock step to the left (exposed) and on gravel to the ridge (markings with black dots help you to find the way). Just before the Belvédère the descent begins to the left (entrance marked with a blue no-entry sign and 'Danger') through a scree gully, full of tree trunks, into the Vallon and to the **Calanque d'En Vau** (17). As in Walk 39 you pass the **Calanque de Port-Pin** (18) and **Calanque de Port-Miou** (19) on the way to Cassis.

The next morning you can start the traverse of the Calanques over the top (compare the alternative in Walk 42).

The cave: the strip of land to the Calanque de l'Escu. The rock face keeps pushing forward to the sea.

44 Montagne de Marseilleveyre, 432m

Along the boundary of town and mountains, and then down to the sea

La Madrague de Montredon – Sommet de Béouveyre – Sommet de Marseilleveyre – Col de la Selle – Calanque de Marseilleveyre – Callelongue

Location: Marseille, Gare Saint-Charles.

Starting point: La Madrague de Montredon (20m) in the southwest corner of Marseille. Best reached with the regular no.19 bus service from Métro Castellane via Métro Rond Point du Prado; both Métro stations are on the red underground line which also goes to the Gare St-Charles.

Destination: Callelongue (0m); small fishing village at the end of the road along the bay from Marseille into the Calanques. No. 20 bus to La Madrague de Mentredon (with a connection to the no.19).

Walking times: La Madrague – Sommet de Marseilleveyre 1¼ hours, descent into the Calanque de Marseilleveyre 1 hour, return to Callelongue ¾ hour. Total time 3 hours.

Ascent: About 550m.

Distance: 8km.

Grade: Between red and black – so you must really be sure-footed and have a head for heights and you need to use your hands now and then.

Best time of year: All year round except high summer.

Refreshments: Restaurants in La Madrague, Calanque de Marseilleveyre (not always open), Callelongue.

Accommodation: In Marseille-Montredon: Hôtel Le Mistral, 31 avenue de la Pointe Rouge, tel: 04 91 73 44 69 (with the no.19 bus from La Madrague). Otherwise in Marseille: Gîte de Marseille – Bonneveine, tel: 04 91 73 97 23; Auberge de Jeunesse de Bonneveine, 47 avenue Vidal, tel: 04 91 73 21 81; Camping Municipal de Bonneveine, tel: 04 91 73 26 99 (none of them far from Bonneveine Plage, no. 10 bus).

Alternative: 1) If the Mistral is blowing at 100 kilometres an hour it is recommended that you take the direct ascent from Callelongue through the yellow-marked Vallon de Miougranier where you have to climb the slightly exposed Escaliers des Géants for a short way; 1¼ hours. 2) On the *Sentier du Président* (compare Walk 42) from Callelongue back to La Madrague; 1¼ hours. 3) Continue from the Col de la Selle along the *Sentier des Crêtes*, which goes up to Cap Morgiou, as far as the Col de Cortiou and return past the Calanque de l'Escu into the Calanque de Marseilleveyre (compare Walks 43 and 45); a marvellous 2¼ hour detour.

Places of Interest: Marseille and the Mediterranean.

Map: IGN 1:15 000: Les Calanques de Marseille à Cassis (3615).

Tip: The view from the Sommet de Marseilleveyre already has three stars. But on the 29th October and 22nd February, at sunset and if there is no mist, the Canigou begins to emerge in the eastern Pyrenees.

Adjoining walks: 42, 43, 45.

The town: Marseille from the Sommet de Marseilleveyre. The Mistral blows often and with surprising force.

The Montagne de Marseilleveyre towers up at the southern edge of Marseille. This powerful craggy massif forms the western part of the Calanques. Its highest summit is the Sommet de Marseilleveyre (432m). A bientôt – see you here and on other mountains inland from the Côte d'Azur.

From the no. 19 bus terminus in **La Madrague de Montredon** go southwards uphill on the coastal road until the hikers' paths begin on the left (amongst others the *GR 51-98*; information board). Go through a holiday park, then steeply up to the Crête de l'Escalette (138m). The black as well as red and white-marked *Sentier du Président* branches off right here. Stay on the blue-marked path *'Corniche Bleu'* from which, after 100m, the brown-marked route *'Corniche Salis'* turns off to the right. Mostly on the north side of the western ridge, the often narrow and exposed path leads up to the **Sommet de Béouveyre** (368m). Go steeply down to the **Col des Chèvres** (312m) – a cable helps the descent through a chimney. At first on the right and then on the left hand side of the ridge go along the path still marked blue, to the **Sommet de Marseilleveyre**. Remains of buildings litter the summit. The blue-marked route descends at first over the north flank, then straight over the eastern ridge down to the **Col de la Selle**. Now go towards the sea on the yellow-marked mountain path which winds down below the towers of the Pointe Callot and the Tête de la Mounine along the right hand side of the Grand Malvallon valley. Just below the Col de la Galinette go left along the yellow-spotted path down into the valley and to the **Calanque de Marseilleveyre**. Walk along the often busy *Sentier de la Douane* to **Callelongue**.

Côte d'Azur: coast of the Alps

'He not only knows all these daughters of the sun, he loves them and looks after them so that we love them too.' With such foresight in December 1887, Figaro discussed the book with a pioneering title, simply *La Côte d'Azur*. This concept for the southeast Mediterranean coast of France had been invented by Stéphen Liégeard (1830-1925), 'an insignificant poet with the best connections', as Mary Blume remarked in her book *Côte d'Azur* in a hardly flattering way. Liégeard lived for decades in Cannes in the Villa Les Violettes and gave his town the title of 'favourite daughter of the sun'.

La Côte d'Azur: 114 years after it was given its name, 'the azure-blue coast' still has a good ring to it. Only a few people know that walkers experience quite a different coast – away from the commotion, but not right away from the problems and not at all away from its beauty. Only if you venture onto the footpaths, onto the *sentiers pédestres*, will you see and understand why Liégeard's strip of land was considered to be paradise on earth.

Gorse and strawberry trees, olive trees and mimosa bushes, villages and villas, mule paths and non-paths, bays and summits, views inland and out to sea. Here there's an amazingly diverse nature in spite of the over-development – a former (agri)culture in harmony with a brick-built nature. You can't

Au revoir: view back from St-Tropez peninsula of the snow-capped Maritime Alps.

always say that about the tourist industry! And then there's the scent of the paths as well which immerse themselves in dense undergrowth, into a richly aromatic landscape. This is walking with your nose and eyes. Grasse, the town of perfume, and Vence, the town of artists will welcome you – many times in many places – that's if you are on foot as Liégeard was too. The Boulevard de la Croisette in Cannes, the Promenade des Anglais in Nice: how beautiful it must have been when there were no urban motorways.

'Les Balcons de la Côte d'Azur' is the name of the *GR 51* long distance path. It has a good ring to it, like the coast, but sometimes it clanks quite loudly when it goes into the developed areas of the Côte d'Azur. What's more there are 508km of connecting footpaths. We've added variety by linking a few official paths to other delightful walking titbits (amongst others of course). And we take the train, the bus and even the boat.

'Next year I will drive to the sea!' You can hear this favourite saying of the French when holidays in the mountains have fallen through again while the sun shone on southern skies. Mountains and sea – they don't seem compatible. Not so in the Calanques, or anywhere else on the Côte d'Azur for that matter, which is actually nothing more than the coast of the Alps. L'année prochaine, j'irai à la mer. Why not now? En route, mes amis!

45 The blue horizon

In 15 stages from Menton to Marseille

Menton – Nice – Grasse – Cannes – Saint-Tropez – Porquerollos – Toulon – Bandol – Marseille

Starting point: Menton-Garavan: first or last stop on French soil for the Nice-Ventimiglia line, but only local trains stop.

Transfer: Rail, bus and boat services connect each section. The *Guide régional des transports* available in larger stations is very useful for the frequently used Menton-Marseille line. It is recommended that you find out in advance the departure times of the various forms of transport.

Destination: Marseille.

Walking times: 86 hours. (5¾ hours a day).

Ascent: 10440m, descent 10170m (about 700m a day).

Distance: 257km (17km a day).

Grade: For hill walkers with coastal experience and sure-footed beach walkers. If you can't walk for hours to fantastic bays and viewing platforms, you will break out in a sweat. If you can't see further than two deckchairs away, you will not find your way on most of the marked paths.

Best time of year: April to June, Sept. to Oct. You risk finding places for accommodation closed in the autumn. In the low season the daily crossing to Porquerolles is not guaranteed, except from La Tour Fondue.

Map: Didier & Richard: 1:50.000 with randonnées pédestres, sheets 24 (Collines provençales), 25 (Les Maures et le Haut Pays Varois), 26 (Au Pays d'Azur). IGN TOP 25: 1:25.000, 3742 OT, 3643 ET, 3544 ET, 3545 OT, 3446 OT, 3245 OT. IGN 1:15 000: Les Calanques (3615). For the Maures alternative 8th and 9th stage: IGN série bleue 1:25.000 3445 E, TOP 25: 3446 ET.

Alternative: Thanks to public transport some stages can be omitted so that you can get from Menton to Marseille in 8 days. On the other hand, you can just do individual sections, eg. the path from Menton to Grasse, or the coastal trek from St-Tropez to Marseille.

Tip: You must take a torch for the Aqueduc de Foulon (6th stage) which goes frequently through a tunnel. Perhaps a mat for the bivouac on Cap Morgiou, but you don't have to have a sleeping bag – or on the last night either.

Places of Interest: The azure-blue coast from a walker's perspective.

1st stage: Menton-Garavan – Ste-Agnès

5½ hours. Ascent 1280m, descent 620m. 15km. *Route: GR 51 of the balcons de la Côte d'Azur*. From Ste-Agnès to the Château de Haroun (766m) on the rock above the village. Walk 4. *Accommodation:* Saint-Yves, tel: 04 93 35 91 45.

2nd stage: Ste-Agnès – Èze-Bord-de-Mer (– Nice)

6¾ hours. Ascent 800m, descent 1450m. 18km. *Route: GR 51* to Col de Guerre. Mont de la Bataille (620m) – La Turbie – Cime de la Forna (621m) – Maison de la Nature – Èze-Village – Èze-Bord-de-Mer. Local train to Nice.

Walk 5. *Accommodation*: in Èze-Bord-de-Mer: Eric Rivot, tel: 04 93 01 51 46; in Nice: Negresco, tel: 04 93 88 39 51, and many more reasonable, eg. Locarno, Primotel Suisse, Berne, Frank Zurich, Helvétique, Interlaken.

3rd stage: (Nice –) Cantaron – Aspremont

4½ hours. Ascent 1000m, descent 600m. 13km. *Route:* Local train from Nice central station, direction Sospel to Cantaron. *GR 51* to Baisse de Rougier. Mont Macaron (806m) – Ruines de Châteauneuf – Col de Châteauneuf –Tourrette-Levens. GR 51 to Baisse de Rougier. Mont Macaron (806m) – Ruines de Châteauneuf – Col de Châteauneuf – Tourrette-Levens. GR 51 to Aspremont. *Alternative*: all on the *GR 51* without Mont Macaron 1½ hours shorter. Walks 9, 10. *Accommodation*: Aspremont, tel: 04 93 08 00 05; Saint-Jean, tel: 04 93 08 00 66.

4th stage: Aspremont – St-Jeannet

5¼ hours. Ascent 780m, descent 850m. 15km. *Route: GR 51* via La Manda (stop for the 'fir cone train' Nice-Digne) and Gattières to signpost 18 above Gattières. La Colle (842m) – Le Gros Chêne – Baou de la Gaude (796m) – Vallon de Parriau – St-Jeannet. *Alternative*: without Baou de la Gaude 1 hour shorter. Walk 11. *Accommodation*: Gîte d'étape, tel: 04 93 24 87 11; Sainte-Barbe, tel: 04 93 24 94 38.

5th stage: St-Jeannet – St-Barnabé

5 hours. Ascent 940m, descent 400m. 18km. *Route: GR 51*. *Alternative*: detour from the Vallon de Parriau to the Baou de St-Jeannet (800m). Walk 11. *Accommodation*: in St-Barnabé: Gîte d'étape St-Martin, tel: 04 93 59 11 66. In Courmes: Auberge, tel: 04 93 77 64 70.

6th stage: St-Barnabé – Grasse (– Cannes)

7 hours. Ascent 200m, descent 830m. 21km. *Route: GR 51* to signpost 86 at La Baisse. Westwards to Pré Royer/signpost 154, steeper descent to the Pont de Bramafan. GR 51 along the aqueduct from Foulon (with a diversion) to the northern edge of Grasse. Through the town to the Gare Routière (tel: 04 93 36 49 61 or 04 93 36 37 37) and by bus to Cannes. *Alternative: GR 51* via Courmes, with direct descent into th small village. Walks 12, 15. *Accommodation:* in Grasse: La Printania, tel: 04 93 36 95 00. In Cannes: from the Festival to the Estival; good: Pullmann, tel: 04 93 38 62 91.

7th stage: (Cannes –) Théoule-sur-Mer – Anthéor-Plage (– St-Raphaël)

8 hours. Ascent and descent both 1100m. 20km. *Route:* local train to Théoule-sur-Mer. *GR 51* to Col de la Cadière. Sommet des Grosses Grues (441m) – Sommet des Petites

Grues (411m) – Pic de l'Ours (492m) – Pic d'Aurelle (322m) – Pic du Cap Roux (453m) – Col du St-Pilon – Plateau d'Anthéor – Anthéor-Plage. Local train or bus to St-Raphaël (Info: tel: 04 94 95 16 71). Walk 20. *Accommodation*: in Théoule-sur-mer: Grand Hôtel, tel: 04 93 49 96 04; Auberge de Jeunesse de Trayas below the Col Notre-Dame, tel: 04 93 75 40 23. In Anthéor: Les Flots Bleus, tel: 04 94 44 80 21. In St-Raphaël: Les Amandiers, tel: 04 94 19 85 30; Auberge de Jeunesse de Fréjus, tel: 04 94 52 18 75.

8th stage: (St-Raphaël –) St-Tropez – Plage de l'Escalet
6 hours. Ascent and descent both 250m. 23km. *Route:* from St-Raphaël by bus (Sodetrav, tel: 04 94 12 55 00) to St-Tropez. *Sentier littoral* round Cap de St-Tropez and Cap Camarat. Walks 27, 28. *Accommodation*: in St-Tropez: Le Colombier, tel: 04 94 97 05 31. On the Plage de Tahiti: La Ferme d'Augustin, tel: 04 94 97 23 83. In L'Escalet: L'Amphore, tel: 04 94 12 90 90; Camping Caravaning La Cigale (with bungalows), tel: 04 94 79 22 53.

9th stage: Plage de l'Escalet – Cavalaire-sur-Mer
5 hours. Ascent and descent both 500m. 15km. *Route: sentier littoral* round Cap Lardier. *Alternative*: only to La Croix-Valmer-Plage and from there take the boat to Porquerolles. And: also from Cavalaire-sur-Mer on the same day to Porquerolles, perhaps via La Tour Fondue. Walk 28. *Accommodation*: in Cavalaire: Bellevue, tel: 04 94 64 01 38; Raymond, tel: 04 94 64 07 32; Alpazur, tel: 04 94 64 01 02. In La-Croix-Valmer: La Ricarde, tel: 04 94 79 64 07.

10th stage: (Cavalaire-sur-Mer –) Porquerolles
6 hours. Ascent and descent both 600m. 20km. *Route:* by boat from Cavalaire to Porquerolles; Compagnie des Transports Maritimes Vedettes Îles d'Or, tel: 04 94 79 53 06 or 04 94 71 01 02. Or by bus from Cavalaire to Hyères Gare Routière (Info Sodetrav, tel: 04 94 12 55 00), change buses to La Tour Fondue and by boat in 20 min. to Porquerolles (Transport Littoral Varois, tel: 04 94 58 21 81). Walk on sometimes narrow and hidden coastal path round Porquerolles island: Plage d'Argent – Anse Bon Renaud – Pointe de l'Aiguade – Calanque du Maure with the pirates' hole – Pointe du Grand Langoustier – northwards past the Mas du Langoustier – Pointe des Carrières – Calanque du Brégançonnet – Mont de Tiélo (108m) – Gorges du Loup – Phare de

Porquerolles –Pointe de l'Oustau de Diéu – Mont des Salins (127m) – Plage Notre-Dame – Fort de l'Alycastre – Plage de la Courtade – Porquerolles. *Alternative:* instead of walking, go round the island on mountainbike – or just wheel down to the next beach. Walk 31. *Accommodation*: Auberge les Glycines, tel: 04 94 58 30 36; Sainte Anne, tel: 04 94 58 30 04; Café Porquerollais, tel:

04 94 12 32 70.

11th stage: (Porquerolles – Toulon –) Fabrégas – Sanary-sur-Mer
7 hours. Ascent and descent 400m. 20km. *Route:* 2 possibilities from Porquerolles to Toulon: 1) direct by boat (Le Batelier de la Rade, tel: 04 94 46 24 65; Transmed 2000 Monarque, tel: 04 94 92 96 82; sometimes no service and sometimes only eve-

nings, so you might have to stay overnight in Toulon or Fabrégas). 2) via Hyères (boat to La Tour Fondue, bus to Hyères Gare SNCF, local train to Toulon). From the Place de la Liberté in Toulon with no. 8 bus, 189 or 198 to La Seyne-sur-Mer; change in Seyne-Centre to the 83 to Fabrégas. *Sentier littoral* round Cap Sicié with its highest point, the Notre-Dame du Mai (358m), to Le Brusc Port and continue along the coast to Sanary-sur-Mer. *Alternative*: from Le Brusc Port by bus via the Sauviou crossroads (change buses) to Sanary. Walk 35. *Accommodation*: in Fabrégas: L'Esteleto, tel: 04 94 94 84 40. In Sanary: La Walk, tel: 04 94 74 10 10. In Bandol: Plein Large, tel: 04 94 32 23 32.

12th stage: (Sanary-sur-Mer –) Bandol – St-Cyr-sur-Mer (– La Ciotat)
4 hours. Ascent and descent 200m. 14km. *Route:* bus to Bandol. To the Plage de Renécros; *sentier littoral* round the Pointe du Défens to La Madrague; road to St-Cyr-sur-Mer. Local train to La Ciotat; bus or on foot to the harbour; perhaps also bus from Les Lecques to La Ciotat. Walk 36. *Accommodation*: La Rotonde, tel: 04 42 08 67 50.

13th stage: La Ciotat – Cassis
5 hours. Ascent and descent 650m. 14km. *Route:* at first a detour to the Parc du Mugel uand Belvédère du Large, then coastal path via Montagne de la Canaille and Sémaphore du Bec de l'Aigle (322m), La Grande Tête (394m), Pointe des Vanades (344m), Cap Soubeyran (348m) and Cap Canaille (363m) to Cassis. *Alternative:* without Belvédère du Large. *Accommodation*: Le Clos des Arômes, tel: 04 42 01 71 84; Le Grand Jardin, tel: 04 42 01 70 10; Auberge de Jeunesse La Fontasse, tel: 04 42 01 02 72.

14th stage: Cassis – Cap Morgiou
6½ hours. Ascent and descent 930m. 18km. *Route:* GR 51 via Falaise du Devenson (318m) to the Col du Renard; and out onto Cap Morgiou. Walks 39, 41, 42. *Accommodation*: between Cassis (ie. the youth hostel) and La Madrague near Marseille there is no accommodation. 3 possibilities: 1) combine the 14th and 15th stages (one section shorter without the detour to Cap Morgiou!). 2) break the walk at the Université de Luminy (5 hours from Cassis) and take one of the frequent no. 21 buses to Marseille, stay overnight, for example, in the Hotel Le Corbusier in the Cité Radieuse, 280

Boulevard Michelet (bus stops right in front), tel: 04 91 77 18 15, fax: 04 91 71 09 93 and resume your walk the next day in Luminy. 3) camping in the Calanques is forbidden, but a bivouac on the way, eg. at Cap Morgiou, is allowed and dine in Morgiou (check beforehand to see if the Nautic Bar is open; tel: 04 91 40 06 37) and have breakfast in Sormiou.

15th stage: Cap Morgiou – La Madrague/Marseille

5 hours. Ascent and descent 800m. 13km. *Route: GR 51* to Col de Cortiou. Blue-marked *Sentier des Crêtes* via Tête de l'Homme (396m), Sommet Ouest de l'Homme Mort (374m), Sommet de Marseilleveyre (432m) and Sommet de Béouveyre (368m) to La Madrague de Montredon: rien ne va plus. By bus 19 (last bus at 21.30) to Métro Rond Point du Prado and by underground to Marseille Gare St-Charles. *Alternative*: instead of going down to Sormiou continue straight over the ridge and then down to the GR on the Col des Baumettes. Walks 42, 44. *Accommodation*: in Marseille-Montredon: Hôtel Le Mistral, 31 avenue de la Pointe Rouge, tel: 04 91 73 44 69; also by bus 19: Auberge de Jeunesse de Bonneveine, 47 avenue Vidal, tel: 04 91 73 21 81.

Alternative 8th stage: (St-Raphaël –) Pignans – Collobrières

4¾ hours. Ascent and descent 600m. 13km. *Route:* from St-Raphaël by train or bus (Info tel: 04 94 12 55 00 or 04 94 53 78 46) to Pignans. GR9 to Notre-Dames des Anges (767m), GR 90 to Collobrières. *Accommodation*: Hôtel Notre Dame, tel: 04 94 48 07 13, Auberge des Maures, tel: 04 94 48 07 10.

Alternative 9th stage: Collobrières – Bormes-les-Mimosas (– Porquerolles)

9 hours. Ascent and descent 1000m. 30km. *Route: GR 90* to Plateau Lambert. Marked loop via Chartreuse de la Verne (closed tuesdays, Easter, Ascension Day, Whitsun, the Assumption of the Virgin Mary as well as Christmas) and Sommet de l'Argentière to the Noyer-Staubecken. *GR 90* via Maison Rusca to Col de Landon. Pré de Roustan – La Pierre d'Avenon (443m) – Vallon de Landon – Coste Drèche – Bormes-les-Mimosas. The next morning walk 45 min. on the GR 90 to Le Lavandou and take the boat (Vedettes Îles d'Or, tel: 04 94 71 01 02) to Porquerolles; or by bus from Bormes-les-Mimosas or Bormes-Pin via Hyères Gare Routière to La Tour Fondue and boat to Porquerolles. *Alternative*: without Chartreuse de la Verne 1 ¼ hours shorter. Walks 25, 26.

Accommodation: at the Carthusian monastery of Verne: Refuge des Sivadières west of the Sommet de l'Argentière: small hut, always open. Take cooking stove, mattress, sleeping bag as well as water. In Bormes: Grand Hôtel, tel: 04 94 71 23 72. In Le Lavandou: Auberge de la Falaise, tel: 04 94 71 01 35.

Index

The numbers after each entry relate to the Walk numbers. Words like Colle, Mont, Rocher etc. are placed after the name.